More Back of the Box Gourmet

From Spamburgers™ to Toll House® Derby Pies—
A Nostalgic Collection of More Than 120 Hit Recipes
From American Food Packages

Michael McLaughlin

A John Boswell Associates/King Hill Productions Book

SIMON & SCHUSTER
New York London Toronto Sydney Tokyo Singapore

A John Boswell Associates/King Hill Productions Book

SIMON & SCHUSTER
Simon & Schuster Building
Rockefeller Center
1230 Avenue of the Americas
New York, New York 10020

Designed by Barbara Cohen Aronica
Typesetting by Jackson Typesetting in Jackson, MI
Printed in Stevens Point, WI by Worzalla

10 9 8 7 6 5 4 3 2 1

Library of Congress Cataloging-in-Publication Data

McLaughlin, Michael,
    More back of the box gourmet / by Michael McLaughlin.
        p.   cm.
    Includes index.
    ISBN: 0-671-86721-0 : $15.00
    1. Cookery. I. Title.
TX714.M386   1994
641.5—dc20   93-25840
                                                     CIP

To Francine—
What a trip around the kitchen it's been.

CONTENTS

CHAPTER ONE · Feeling Condimental   15
From ketchup to mustard, steak sauce to salsa and every zesty condiment in between, these recipes for dishes from meat loaf to apple pie, from sandwiches to cookies get a special boost of flavor from their spicy secret ingredient.

CHAPTER TWO · From the Beverage Cart   27
A splash of sweet liqueur, a cup of strong coffee, a few spoonfuls of good bourbon, a measure of freshly brewed tea or a sprinkle of Tang®—all add sparkle to convenient, home-style recipes for drinks, desserts, main dishes, stuffings and more.

CHAPTER THREE · The Cereal Aisle   39
Not just for breakfast any more, healthful, high-fiber cereals of all kinds have become the secret ingredient in treats ranging from snack mixes to chocolate chip cookies, from main courses to sweet dessert bars.

CHAPTER FOUR · The Candy Jar   49
They're easy treats for people on the move and we love to eat them plain, but our favorite candies, caramels and bars (not to mention marshmallows) can also add a secret sweet something to cakes, puddings, pies, cookies and more.

CHAPTER FIVE · Beans, Grains and Pasta   57
Carbohydrate lovers have cause for celebration. Good-for-you and good-to-eat noodles, beans and grains are the main ingredient in these hearty casseroles, side dishes, soups, main courses. And for dessert there's an old-fashioned rice pudding.

CHAPTER SIX · Peanut Butter and Jelly   69
There's not a kid's lunchbox sandwich in sight, but together or separately, our all-time favorite American flavor duo stars in everything from appetizers to cakes, from pasta sauce to rich ice cream toppings.

A LIST OF THE RECIPES BY CATEGORY

Sweet and Sour Chicken, 100
Crisp Chicken Drumsticks, 126
Polynesian Stuffed Chicken Breasts, 128
Country Herb Roasted Chicken, 133
Classic Herb Chicken, 48
Wild Rice Chicken Supreme, 65
Buffalo Wings, 81
Honey Mustard Chicken Sandwiches, 83

SEAFOOD

Seafood Enchilada Casserole, 116
Scampi A La Di Saronno®, 30
Fish au Gratin, 78
Crab Cakes, 121

PORK AND HAM

Baby Back Ribs with Spiced Apple Glaze, 23
Roast Pork Calypso, 33
Pork Chops 'n Peaches, 124
Red Beans and Rice, 132
Sausage and Pancake Bake, 130
Apple-Glazed Ham Loaf, 44

BEEF

Steak Pot Pie, 24
Cincinnati Chili, 37
Swiss Steak De Lombardi, 114
Oven-Barbecued Beef Brisket, 139

Barbecue Meatloaf, 22
Vegetable Meatloaf, 135
Manhattan Meatballs, 75
Shortcut Sloppy Joes, 137

VEGETABLES AND BEANS

Scalloped Corn, 45
California Bean Bake, 66
Maple Glazed Sweet Potatoes, 99
Gourmet Green Beans, 131
Savory Mashed Potatoes, 140
Golden Corn & Green Bean Bake, 136
Refried Black Beans, 68
Lentil Soup, 67
Layered Bean Dip, 58
Broccoli 'n Rice Casserole, 62
Refrigerator Pickles, 129
Sunny Potato Salad, 18
Seven-Layer Salad, 77
Pine-Apple Coleslaw, 82
Cool 'n Creamy Coleslaw, 98
Red Beans and Rice, 132

BREADS AND BREADSTUFFS

Country Dijon Wheat Bread, 25
Cranberry Pecan Stuffing, 32
Cinnamon Date Nut Bread, 97
Mexicorn® Spoon Bread, 117
Hush Puppies, 63

PIES, COBBLERS AND PASTRIES

Love Apple Pie, 20
Easy Grasshopper Pie, 52
Toffee Fantasy Pie, 53
Toll House® Derby Pie, 88
Pecan Pie, 101
Classic Crisco® 9-Inch Double Crust, 105
Lattice-Topped Raisin Pie, 106
"Philly" Pastry, 104
Nilla® Cranapple Crisp, 125

CAKE

Cherry Coffee Cake, 55
Peanut Butter and Jelly Swirl Bundt Cake, 71
Southern Jam Cake, 72
Amaisin Raisin Cake, 79
Sock-It-To-Me Cake, 108
Orange Kiss-Me Cake, 107
Pineapple Upside Down Cake, 112
"Philly" Pound Cake, 103
Delicate Graham Cracker Cake, 123
Lemon Chiffon Cake, 94
Kraut Conquers All Chocolate Cake, 115

COOKIES AND BARS

Hot 'n Nutty Cookies, 16
Classic Shortbread with Drambuie® Glaze, 31

Wheatena® Chocolate Chip Cookies, 42
Cherry Dot Cookies, 40
Melting Moments, 90
S'Mores, 122
Choco-Peanut Bars, 89
Zebra Brownies, 93
Rich Lemon Bars, 138
Butterfinger™ Cookies, 56

CHOCOLATE

"Grand Indulgence" Hot Chocolate, 28
Deep Dark Chocolate Cake, 86
Red Velvet Cocoa Cake, 87
Kraut Conquers All Chocolate Cake, 115
Zebra Brownies, 93
Chocolate Scotcheroos, 43
Chocolate Caramel Nut Bars, 51
Choco-Peanut Bars, 89
Chocolate Dessert Sauce, 50
Chocolate Peanut Butter Sauce, 74

PUDDINGS AND SHERBETS

Old Fashioned Ambrosia Pudding, 119
Creamy Milky Way® Bar Pudding, 50
Old Fashioned Rice Pudding, 64
Lemon Tea Sherbet, 34

ICINGS, FROSTINGS AND TOPPINGS

Maple Frosting, 72
One-Bowl Buttercream Frosting, 86
Fluffy Vanilla Frosting, 87
Lemon Glaze, 94
Toffee Blanket, 38
Peanut Butter Sauce, 74
Toasted Coconut Pineapple Peanut Butter Sauce,
   74

SAUCES, GLAZES AND DRINKS

Kahlúa® Barbecue Sauce, 36
Sweet 'n Spicy Glaze, 80
Basic Barbeque Sauce, 96
Orient Express Stir-Fry Sauce, 100
Russian Tea Mix, 35

INTRODUCTION

Walk slowly down the hall with me, take a right turn, open the door and there it is—a modern American kitchen cupboard full of the cans, jars, bottles and boxes that make up so much of what we eat each night. It is a pantry full of promise, and I'm delighted to be setting out once again in exploration of what goes on here on the back of the box. The shelves of this cupboard are well stocked with mayonnaise and peanut butter, dried soup mix and salad dressing, lemon juice from concentrate and fruit cocktail, steak sauce and coffee liqueur. Each has a primary use for which it was designed by the manufacturer and for which it was purchased by the owner, of course, but there are other, more entertaining, possibilities.

Thanks to the creative (and tireless) minds in the test kitchens of food corporations across the country, you may, if you so choose, use your soup mix in a meat loaf, your steak sauce in a potpie, your breakfast cereal in a cocktail snack. The goal for the corporate kitchen in question is primarily to get you to use more of the ingredient (certainly to impress you with the multiple possibilities), but the by-product of this effort when it works well is a kind of harmless kitchen entertainment that people seem to love. (You mean there's tomato soup or mayonnaise or sauerkraut in *this* cake?!) With the recipes from the back of the box (can, jar, bottle, package) every cook can be a minor kitchen magician, transforming rab-

bits into doves, so to speak, merely with the flick of a spoon, knife, fork or can opener.

This is my second visit to back-of-the-box land, and in many ways it's been an eye opener. The first collection of these hearty, home-style convenience recipes I assembled four years ago concentrated on the venerable classics. There were, after all, recipes that had appeared on boxes for over fifty years, had stood the test of time, had become nostalgic home cooking for many, and most of which had, judging from my personal reaction, been cooked at one time or another by my own mother. No longer merely promotional tools, they had become a part of the national food consciousness. (When I think American Cookie I think of a Nestlé's® Toll House®, and so, apparently, do millions of other people.) The response to the book was about what I expected—enthusiasm evenly divided between those who just wanted to read and think about familiar foods from their past and those who had to get dinner on the table tonight and were looking for help, quick, proving that the next generation's fond food memories are simmering away on the tops of stoves all over the country right now.

Of course, some classics were overlooked last time, something I learned on the road when over and over people asked for their favorite back-of-the-box recipe only to hear I had somehow missed it. Amaisin Raisin Cake, moist with luscious Hellmann's®/Best Foods® mayonnaise, those bar cookies with German chocolate cake mix and Kraft® caramels, that glazing mixture composed of Lipton® soup mix, Russian dressing and apricot preserves, the two-ingredient barbecue sauce from the Grandma's® molasses jar, Kellogg's® Chocolate Scotcheroos—where were they all?

So I set out to fill in some of these gaps in the list of classics, to borrow recipes from even more food corporations than before and to continually look for those that used the ingredients in question in offbeat and creative ways, but always with the goal of also producing something good to eat. I found all these secrets and more, and along the way also learned a lot about how these products—many of them a part of our daily lives for so many years we no longer give them another thought—were originally devised and developed.

As someone who sometimes writes seriously about serious food, I am often asked how it's possible for me to also be interested in these fast, convenient and decidedly non-"gourmet" dishes. Aside from the fact that I grew up eating many of them and don't seem any the worse for the wear, my answer, as always, is that it's not possible to talk to people about what they *should* be eating if you're not familiar with what they ate growing up or what they are eating right now. Read on, gourmets, if you want to uncover a few secrets of your own.

A NOTE ON THE RECIPES

As in my first back-of-the-box collection, the texts of these recipes have been printed verbatim, exactly as provided to me by the food companies. (Modernizations—microwave, food processor, low fat, etc.—sometimes occur, but there is much at stake, and test kitchen disasters are rare. Even in remodeled recipes the essential old-fashioned quality of the original survives.) Under the heading "Gilding the Lily" I have again suggested possible changes that may interest you. Readers of the first book welcomed these simple touches that were intended to add flair to beloved classics, and I hope you will, too.

1

FEELING CONDIMENTAL

Condiments—those tangy sauces we splash on food for an instant boost of flavor—have been around for centuries. One of the earliest was called *garum*. Produced in ancient Rome, *garum* consisted of the liquid poured off after small fish, fish entrails and oysters were salted and allowed to decay in the sun for several days. (Wine, honey, spices, herbs or vinegar were added, depending on how the condiment was to be used.) One is inclined at first to reconsider the glory that was Rome, until, flashing forward to the present, we read on the Worcestershire sauce label that its contents include molasses, anchovies and/or sardines, chili peppers and tamarind—the tart fruit pod of a leguminous tree native to India. Condiment-wise, things do not seem to have changed all that much in the past two thousand years, which is probably why these recipes sound so tangy and good.

HOT 'N NUTTY COOKIES

One hundred and twenty-five years after Edmund McIlhenny first concocted the hot pepper sauce that has come to be called Tabasco®, his descendants still make this quintessential condiment. Located on Avery Island, a salt mountain rising out of the Louisiana bayou, the company crushes red ripe, Central America–grown hot peppers, mixes them with salt mined from the island and ages the potent mash that results in white oak barrels for up to three years. The fiery puree is then blended with vinegar and stirred frequently for weeks before being strained and bottled. While a dash or two will enliven almost any dish, these double nutty cookies are a particularly unusual but otherwise delicious application of the hot stuff.

¾ cup unsalted butter, softened
1 cup granulated sugar
1 cup packed brown sugar
2 cups peanut butter, smooth or crunchy
½ cup macadamia nuts, chopped (optional)
2 eggs
1 teaspoon vanilla extract
1 teaspoon TABASCO® Pepper Sauce
3 cups all-purpose flour
1 teaspoon salt
1 teaspoon baking soda

Preheat oven to 350°F. Lightly butter and flour a cookie sheet.

In a large bowl, cream together butter and sugars. Stir in peanut butter and macadamia nuts; mix until well blended. Add eggs, vanilla, and TABASCO® Pepper Sauce. Mix until well combined.

In another bowl, mix together flour, salt and baking soda. Add to nut mixture and stir until blended.

Spoon about 1 heaping tablespoon of batter on prepared cookie sheet. Coat the tines of a fork in flour and score each cookie in a crisscross pattern. Bake 15–17 minutes, or until edges begin to turn golden. Set aside to cool on racks.

MAKES 2 DOZEN COOKIES.

GILDING THE LILY: Other nuts (particularly pecans) can be successfully substituted. Most TABASCO® recipes call for fairly modest amounts of what is, in fact, quite a hot hot sauce; resist the temptation to add more to these cookies, however—the heat level is just right.

SUNNY POTATO SALAD

Gulden's® was founded over one hundred and thirty years ago, producing as many as thirty different types of mustard from its original plant on Elizabeth Street, near New York City's South Street Seaport. There ships brought in the mustard seed, vinegar and other spices (they're secret—don't ask) that contribute to Gulden's® quality. Today there are three Gulden's® mustards—Golden Yellow, Hot Diablo and Spicy Brown—and the family-owned business has been sold to a national conglomerate, but the quality remains high, and the mustard remains an essential ingredient, particularly when it comes to a summertime batch of this picnic potato salad.

6 medium potatoes (about 2 pounds), boiled, peeled and thickly sliced
1 small onion, chopped
1 medium tomato, chopped
½ cup chopped celery
2 slices bacon, cooked and crumbled
½ cup mayonnaise
⅓ cup GULDEN'S® Special Blend Yellow Mustard
2 tablespoons tarragon vinegar
2 tablespoons sugar, or to taste

Combine potatoes, onion, tomato, celery and bacon. Blend mayonnaise, mustard, vinegar and sugar. Spoon dressing over potato salad; toss gently to coat. Refrigerate until ready to use.

MAKES 6 SERVINGS.

CHICKEN ROMANO

Chili sauce (which contains no chilies) is a bit of a mystery, condimentally speaking. Aside from making an impromptu Thousand Island–type dressing, just what is it for? Some mix it with horseradish to make classic red cocktail dip for cold boiled shrimp, but ketchup works almost as well. It can top a meat loaf, and some people use it on a hamburger, but usually only when they are out of ketchup. Is it only ketchup's bumpy twin or what? Why do they make the stuff, anyway? And why do I buy it? Well, one use for chili sauce is this easy recipe, which requires rather a lot of it to produce a tasty, vaguely Italian glaze for sautéed chicken—a quick and easy supper dish and at least one answer to the mystery.

2 to 2½ pounds broiler-fryer chicken pieces
2 tablespoons vegetable oil
Salt
Pepper
1 medium onion, halved, sliced
1 bottle (12 ounces) HEINZ® Chili Sauce
1 teaspoon dried oregano leaves, crushed
Grated Parmesan cheese

In large skillet, brown chicken in oil; drain excess fat. Season chicken with salt and pepper; add onion. Cover; cook 30 minutes. Stir in chili sauce and oregano. Cook, uncovered, 10 minutes, basting frequently. Skim excess fat from sauce. Serve sauce over chicken; sprinkle with cheese.

MAKES 4-5 SERVINGS (about 1½ cups sauce).

GILDING THE LILY: Serve with thin spaghetti tossed with butter, garlic and Parmesan and broil up a batch of garlic bread.

LOVE APPLE PIE

So dominant is "tomato ketchup" (now considered a redundant expression) it's possible to forget there were once other types of the condiment. Originating in China as *ket-tsiap*, a pickled fish sauce, the relish made its way in the early 1700s to England, where mushroom ketchup and other variations livened the stodgy fare. Transplanted to this country, tomato ketchup dominated the national taste buds. First packed in 1876 by F. & J. Heinz, then a Pennsylvania-based horseradish company, ketchup remained America's most popular condiment until 1992, when salsa overtook it.

The name of this streusel-topped pie, with its generous dollop of ketchup, is a culinary pun. Tomatoes, imported to Italy from Mexico, were originally yellow and were called *pommodoro* ("golden apple") by the Italians. The French transformed the word into *pomme d'amour*, or "love apple," which bit of nomenclatural whimsy inspired someone at Heinz® to then combine apples and ketchup. The coupling is no stranger than mayonnaise in cake. Sweet-tart and pinkish red, the pie looks and tastes great.

⅓ cup HEINZ® Tomato Ketchup
2 teaspoons lemon juice
6 cups sliced, peeled firm tart cooking apples
  (about 2 pounds)
⅔ cup all-purpose flour
⅓ cup granulated sugar
1 teaspoon cinnamon
⅓ cup butter or margarine, slightly softened
1 unbaked 9-inch pie shell

Blend ketchup and lemon juice; combine with apples. For topping, combine flour, sugar and cinnamon; cut in butter until well-blended. Fill pie shell with apples; sprinkle topping over apples. Bake in 425°F oven, 35 to 45 minutes until crust is golden and apples are tender.

MAKES 6-8 SERVINGS.

NOTE: If apples are very tart, add 1 to 2 tablespoons granulated sugar to ketchup mixture.

BARBECUE MEATLOAF

Of all the various condiments that can be stirred into or smeared onto a meat loaf on its way to gracing your table, perhaps none has so great a transforming effect as good old barbecue sauce. Far more than ketchup, barbecue sauce adds color, moisture and a considerable touch of smoky, sweet and sour flavor that will have your family according meat loaf new respect. Make the simple substitution the next time you prepare your favorite recipe, or try this easy formula from Kraft®.

1 pound ground beef
½ cup KRAFT® Thick 'N Spicy Original Barbecue
    Sauce or KRAFT® Barbecue Sauce
½ cup old fashioned or quick oats, uncooked
½ cup finely chopped onion
1 egg, beaten

Preheat oven to 375°F.

Mix together all ingredients except ¼ cup barbecue sauce.

Shape into loaf in 12 × 8-inch baking dish. Bake 45 to 50 minutes. Let stand 5 minutes. Top with remaining barbecue sauce.

4 SERVINGS.

VARIATION: Substitute 1 pound LOUIS RICH® Ground Turkey for ground beef.

BABY BACK RIBS WITH SPICED APPLE GLAZE

The appeal of pork paired with fruit can't be denied. Some combinations are cloyingly sweet and may not be to everyone's taste, but this complex and zesty formula, from Heinz®, will please most rib-lovers. Seasoned with a little of this and a little of that, it has the look of a cherished heirloom recipe that has been tinkered with and improved over the years, the kind that was perfected by some grill-loving guy rather than as a test kitchen project. Since Heinz 57 Sauce® contains a measure of apple, its inclusion here makes culinary sense.

⅓ cup chopped onion
1 cup applesauce
¼ cup apple juice
¼ cup apple jelly
½ cup HEINZ 57 SAUCE®
1 tablespoon lemon juice
½ teaspoon dried tarragon leaves
½ teaspoon allspice
Dash hot pepper sauce
⅛ teaspoon garlic powder
6 racks pork baby back ribs (about 6 pounds)
½ cup apple juice
½ teaspoon salt
¼ teaspoon dried tarragon leaves
⅛ teaspoon dried sage

For glaze, combine first 10 ingredients in small saucepan. Cook over medium heat 20 minutes or until thickened, stirring occasionally. Brush ribs with ½ cup apple juice. Combine salt, ¼ teaspoon tarragon and sage. Rub into ribs; let stand 15 minutes. Grill over medium hot coals 20 minutes, turning occasionally and brushing with apple juice. Brush with glaze and continue grilling 5 minutes. Arrange ribs on serving platter and serve with remaining sauce.

MAKES 6–8 SERVINGS.

STEAK POT PIE

For some people the concept of leftover steak has no meaning. Others, confronted by a medium-rare slab of cow that clearly would feed a small village for a week, recognize the prudence of asking for a doggy bag. When your premium steak leftovers total a pound and a half or so (and if they survive midnight raids on the refrigerator), remember this steak sauce–seasoned recipe that will allow you to frugally turn the abundance into a second, savory meal for four.

1 cup chopped onion
2 tablespoons margarine
2 tablespoons all-purpose flour
1½ cups beef broth
½ cup A.1.® Steak Sauce
3 cups diced cooked steak (about 1½ pounds)
2 cups frozen peas and carrots, thawed
Prepared pastry for 2-crust pie

In 2-quart saucepan, over medium-high heat, cook onion in margarine until tender. Blend in flour; cook for 1 minute. Add beef broth and steak sauce; cook and stir until mixture thickens and begins to boil. Stir in steak and peas and carrots. Spoon mixture evenly into 4 (16-ounce) ovenproof individual casseroles.
Roll out and cut pastry
crust to fit over casseroles.

Seal crusts to edges of casseroles. Slit tops of crusts to vent. Bake at 400°F for 25 minutes or until golden brown. Serve warm.

MAKES 4 SERVINGS.

COUNTRY DIJON WHEAT BREAD

Though now manufactured in Oxnard, California, Grey Poupon® originated in Dijon, France, for centuries the home of fine French mustards. There really were a Monsieur Grey and a Monsieur Poupon (their firm was established in 1777), though now it is Monsieur Nabisco® who turns out the fiery yellow condiment. America's passion for mustards other than Ball Park Yellow, which began in the Seventies and flourished during the Eighties, shows no signs of abating in the Nineties, and Grey Poupon® is riding a crest of success (and has released several new mustard flavors). So popular are its television commercials ("Pardon me, but would you have any Grey Poupon?"), it is reported that some limousine rental companies stock a few jars for those passengers who, like Wayne and Garth of *Wayne's World,* want to get into the act. New Yorkers with long memories will recall one restaurant's outrageous mustard ice cream (served alongside pan-fried calf's liver), but this hearty bread, perfect with salad and cheese or in a sandwich, makes much more sense.

1 pkg. dry yeast
¼ cup warm water
2 teaspoons sugar
¼ cup butter (or margarine), melted
½ cup water
1 teaspoon salt
½ cup GREY POUPON® Country Dijon® Mustard
2 cups white flour
1 cup whole wheat flour

Dissolve yeast in warm water. Mix in sugar. Set aside. In large bowl, combine butter, water, salt and mustard. Mix in yeast mixture. Beat in 1 cup flour. Mix in remaining flour. Knead, with additional flour as necessary, 10 minutes or until smooth. Place in greased bowl. Cover. Let rise until double in bulk. Punch down. Shape loaf. Place in greased 8½" × 4½" × 2½" loaf pan or shape into braid. Cover. Let rise until double in bulk. Brush with beaten egg white and water, if desired. Bake in preheated 375°F oven 30 to 35 minutes or until golden brown.

PEANUT BUTTER 'N' BACON SANDWICH

Lea & Perrins Worcestershire Sauce ("The Original") came about, as do many good things, by accident. Two Worcester, England, pharmacists, Mr. Lea and Mr. Perrins, attempted to duplicate a condiment formula brought back from India by a customer of theirs, Sir Marcus Sandys. Judged a failure, the batch was forgotten for an undetermined period, then rechecked. Voilà! The aging process had smoothed and mellowed the sauce, and a classic was born. Like most successful condiments, Lea & Perrins mostly gets used as is, shaken over or stirred into cocktail sauce, bloody Marys, steaks, burgers and eggs. One more unusual use is this odd but delicious little sandwich. Given the ease with which the microwave oven produces crisp perfect bacon, this sandwich ought to be more popular; it's a wonderful quick snack.

¼ cup peanut butter
2 strips crisp bacon, crumbled
2 teaspoons LEA & PERRINS Worcestershire
    Sauce
2 teaspoons instant minced onion
2 slices bread

Combine all ingredients. Spread on slice of bread. Top with second slice.

MAKES 1 SANDWICH.

GILDING THE LILY: I confess to a dislike of instant onion, and so prefer minced fresh onion on this. I also like the bread toasted. Try a cold beer with the sandwich.

2

FROM THE BEVERAGE CART

At some point in the evolution of American culture as we know it, it became not enough merely to drink our moonshine straight from the jug. Cocktails were deemed sophisticated, and formulas—never recipes—for various complicated and colorful drinks became the foundations upon which the reputations of bartenders, restaurants, even hotels were built. As usual, leaving well enough alone was never sufficient, and, there being a long tradition of cooking with alcohol in Europe, back-of-the-bottle recipes soon came forth from bottlers and distillers on this side of the pond. Imbibing may be optional, but everyone has to eat, and a splash of this or a jot of that incorporated into soup, sauce or sweet will eventually require the purchase of another bottle of the product as surely as sipping it over ice. (P.S. This cart also serves tea, juice, coffee and that neon-orange breakfast staple, Tang®. Cheers!)

"GRAND INDULGENCE" HOT CHOCOLATE

The most successful comfort foods take a particular happy moment, usually of childhood, and recreate that feeling of well-being so successfully we can call it up as needed, merely by enjoying the food in question. If after a long-ago skating, sled-riding or snowman-making session, a big mug of real hot chocolate ever warmed you and your icy fingers back to happiness, you'll be glad to know this grown-up version will work a similar magic today.

1 quart milk
Grated zest from 1 large orange
3 sticks cinnamon, or ¼ teaspoon ground cinnamon
4 ounces imported semi- or bittersweet chocolate
6 tablespoons (3 ounces) GRAND MARNIER®
Whipped cream for garnish, optional

In a small saucepan over low heat, slowly scald the milk with the orange zest and cinnamon. Remove the cinnamon sticks, if using.

In a blender, combine the hot milk with the chocolate and GRAND MARNIER®. Cover the blender and blend on slow speed until very smooth, about 30 seconds. (Blend slowly to avoid the mixture running over the blender lid.) Pour immediately into warm mugs and top with whipped cream, if desired.

MAKES 4 TO 6 SERVINGS.

GILDING THE LILY: The recipe doesn't say that the chocolate should be chopped, but things will go more smoothly if you do so. Only someone seriously out of touch with the real spirit of hot chocolate would consider whipped cream to be optional. Apply a generous dollop to each mug and then sprinkle it with shaved chocolate curls for added flavor and visual appeal.

FRANGELICO® GLAZED TURKEY

Hazelnuts (also known as filberts) are among the most aristocratic of nuts, and at holiday time, in the usual crowd of pecan- and walnut-studded recipes, my bread, mushroom and hazelnut turkey stuffing has always stood out. When I ran across this easy turkey glaze, using Frangelico®, the Italian liqueur made from "wild hazelnuts, berries and herbs," I immediately incorporated it into my Thanksgiving menu. Frangelico® really does taste like hazelnuts (as for the "wild," well, who knows?), and the glaze makes for a wonderfully easy, shiny and attractive holiday bird.

12–14 lb. turkey, thawed
⅓ cup apricot jam
⅓ cup FRANGELICO®

After preparing stuffing, stuff and truss turkey. To make glaze, strain jam through a sieve or smooth it in a blender. Add FRANGELICO® and mix well. Use it as your baste throughout the roasting period. Make gravy as usual.

SERVES 6 TO 8.

SCAMPI A LA DI SARONNO

"Scampi," which although frequently translated as "loads of garlic with added shrimp" actually refers to the jumbo crustaceans in question and not to the seasoning possibilities, can be varied, and as shown below, may even be garlic-free. A splash of the classic Italian liqueur known as Amaretto Di Saronno®, plus modest amounts of curry powder and heavy cream, brings fresh excitement to a favorite seafood standby. Note: Although the recipe doesn't specify, smart cooks should opt for shelled and deveined shrimp.

⅔ pound scampi (defrosted)
3 teaspoons shallots or onions (finely diced)
2 tablespoons fresh or canned red peppers (⅛-inch dice)
2 teaspoons Madras curry powder
2 tablespoons white wine
4 teaspoons DI SARONNO® Amaretto
½ pint heavy cream (1 cup)
2 teaspoons parsley (chopped)
1 ounce split almonds (toasted until golden brown)
Salt and pepper
2 teaspoons butter

Measure and prepare all ingredients before you begin cooking. Actual cooking time is approx. 10 minutes. Melt butter in heavy frying pan and fry onions or shallots until tender and transparent, but not brown. Add scampi and stir 1 minute. Add white wine and 4 teaspoons sweet peppers. Heat until liquid is reduced by half. Add curry powder and DI SARONNO® Amaretto. Tilt pan toward gas and flame-cook for 30 seconds. Stir in cream and half of the parsley, then cook for 1–2 minutes. Season to taste. If the sauce is too thick, thin with more white wine. Transfer to a warmed serving dish and decorate with the toasted almonds plus the remaining sweet peppers and chopped parsley. Serve with a dish of rice.

SERVES 2.

GILDING THE LILY: Sauté a peeled and minced clove of garlic (but just one!) along with the shallots or onions.

Reprinted by permission of The Paddington Corporation.

CLASSIC SHORTBREAD WITH DRAMBUIE® GLAZE

If you believe that the simpler the cookie the better (a retro-radical posture to assume in these days of macadamia chocolate chunkdom), you're probably already a fan of Scottish shortbread. Tasting of little more than good butter and sugar, these cookies can stand only the slightest of embellishments—one such being a smooth and shiny glaze, created with the two-hundred-year-old Scotch whisky–based liqueur known as Drambuie®.

1 cup unsalted butter, softened
½ cup granulated sugar
1¾ cups all-purpose flour
¼ cup cornstarch
¼ teaspoon salt
1 cup confectioners' sugar, sifted
⅓ cup DRAMBUIE®

Cream butter and sugar together until light and fluffy. Sift in flour, cornstarch and salt. Stir just until mixture forms a soft dough. Using lightly floured hands, press dough evenly into a lightly buttered 9-inch round baking pan. With a fork, lightly press around edge of dough. Using the fork, divide the dough into eight wedges, pressing all the way onto the bottom of the pan.

Bake in preheated 350°F oven for 30 to 35 minutes, just until dough begins to brown. (Shortbread will not be crisp, but will firm upon cooling.) Cut through fork markings to form wedges. Cool completely on a rack. Remove wedges carefully from pan. Whisk confectioners' sugar and DRAMBUIE® until smooth. Spread icing on wedges and let set. Store in airtight container.

MAKES 8 SERVINGS.

GILDING THE LILY: No gilding, just a warning: "8 servings" means 8 *cookies*. If you think just one of these delicious shortbreads represents a serving, you probably also think a bag of potato chips feeds six. Get real.

CRANBERRY PECAN STUFFING

The smooth, slightly woody, slightly nutty taste of Maker's Mark®—a premium sour mash whiskey produced on Star Hill Farm, in Loretto, Kentucky—is due to the use of soft winter wheat rather than rye (which would impart a sour taste) in the mash, followed by a lengthy aging in charred white oak barrels. Though the formula isn't old (Maker's Mark® was begun only in 1953), the small-batch distilling method and distinctive red wax–sealed bottles reinforce the image of time-tested reliability. It was developed to be the smoothest-sipping whiskey ever (and it gets my vote), but the delicious taste means it's also a fine ingredient for cooking. A spoonful or two will revitalize a tired pecan pie, and a somewhat more generous quantity adds extra flavor to this holiday stuffing, baked outside the bird, which is also delicious with roast pork or a country ham.

6 slices bacon
1 cup sliced celery
½ cup chopped onion
1 cup dry, seasoned bread cubes
1½ cups cooked wild rice
¾ cup raw cranberries, chopped
¾ cup pecans
1¼ cups beef broth
1 egg, slightly beaten
4 tablespoons MAKER'S MARK®

In skillet, cook bacon until crisp; drain and crumble. Pour off all but 2 tablespoons drippings.

Cook celery and onion in drippings until tender. Combine celery, onion, bread cubes, cooked rice, cranberries, pecans, broth and egg. After mixing thoroughly, add bourbon. If stuffing is dry, add more bourbon or water.

Bake in a round casserole at 350°F for 30 minutes.

MAKES 6 SERVINGS.

ROAST PORK CALYPSO

Tia Maria®, the liqueur based on premium Jamaican Blue Mountain coffee beans, has been produced in the Caribbean for over three hundred years. Though it may be best enjoyed sipped from a small glass while sitting on the fantail of a large yacht cruising the islands, like plain coffee Tia Maria® can also add its complex flavor to a savory entree, as it does here. (Jamaica is also famous for its ginger, and this recipe includes plenty.)

1 bone-in pork loin roast (3½–4 pounds)
1 tablespoon freshly grated ginger
¾ teaspoon salt
¼ teaspoon cloves
¼ teaspoon freshly ground pepper
2 cloves garlic, minced
1 bay leaf, crumbled
2 cups chicken broth
⅔ cup TIA MARIA®
½ cup packed brown sugar mixed with 1 tablespoon TIA MARIA®
½ teaspoon cornstarch dissolved in 1 tablespoon lime juice

Score top, fatty part of roast with sharp knife in diamond pattern. In small bowl, combine ginger, salt, cloves, pepper, garlic and bay leaf; rub mixture over top of roast. Bring roast to room temperature. Place roast, fatty side up, in baking dish with chicken broth and ⅔ cup TIA MARIA®. Roast in 375°F oven for 1½ to 2 hours, basting often. (Allow 30 minutes per pound of meat.) During last 20 minutes of roasting, spread TIA MARIA®/brown sugar mixture over top of roast. Continue roasting and basting until meat thermometer reads 155° to 160°F. (Tent roast with aluminum foil if sugar begins to brown.) Let roast stand 10 minutes before carving.

To Make Sauce: Skim fat from roasting liquid. Measure liquid, and add water to make 1½ cups. Bring liquid and cornstarch to boil in small saucepan over medium heat. Adjust seasonings to taste. Serve over sliced pork.

MAKES 4–6 SERVINGS.

GILDING THE LILY: Serve the roast with black beans, yellow rice and a lettuce and tomato salad; drink Jamaican beer with the meal and sip a Tia Maria® afterward.

LEMON TEA SHERBET

Tea as a flavoring agent, instead of as a beverage, has a long history but not a wide one. Lately there has been something of a resurgence: foods have been smoked over tea, and desserts especially have been flavored with tea. Here is one such example, which produces a brisk and bracing cooler that's delicious on a hot summer day whether served as is or accompanied by an array of fresh fruit and a dollop of unsweetened whipped cream. The gelatine prevents the formation of ice crystals and keeps the sherbet smooth.

2¼ cups strong LIPTON® Tea*
1 cup sugar
1 envelope KNOX® Unflavored Gelatine
¼ cup cold water
¼ cup lemon juice
2 egg whites

*Allow about 4 cup-size Flo-Thru® Tea Bags to 2¼ cups water and prepare according to package directions.

In small saucepan, combine tea with sugar and boil 10 minutes. Soften gelatine in cold water and stir into hot syrup until gelatine is dissolved. Cool, then stir in lemon juice.

In medium bowl, beat egg whites until stiff but not dry. Gradually fold in tea mixture and pour into 2 ice trays. Freeze until almost firm.

Turn into chilled mixer bowl; beat until light and fluffy at low speed, then at high speed. Quickly return to trays, cover with foil, freeze until firm (overnight).

MAKES ABOUT 6 CUPS, OR 12 SERVINGS.

GILDING THE LILY: If you have some sort of ice cream maker (the kind that uses ice and salt is preferable), by all means use it. You won't need to beat the almost-frozen sherbet with the mixer, and the texture will be even smoother.

RUSSIAN TEA MIX

It took ten years to refine and perfect the formula for Tang®, the technological equivalent of fresh orange juice. A decade is not all that long when you consider how much time it must have taken nature to evolve the original model. At first it wasn't even orange; it was a clear drink. Eventually, in 1965, the powdery stuff (now colored a rather dubious shade of orange and packed with vitamins—getting them in was part of General Food's developmental struggles) was marketed. Tang® took off (you should pardon the expression) immediately after NASA decided to send it into space with the Gemini astronauts. Kids insisted on drinking for breakfast on the ground what America's heroes were drinking for breakfast in space. Getting any breakfast product onto our tables later in the day is always a goal of corporate test kitchens; hence this spiced orange instant tea mix, one which lets you whip up everything from a cup to a quart more or less on demand.

1⅓ cups TANG® Orange Flavor Sugar-Sweetened
 Beverage Crystals*
½ cup sugar
⅓ cup instant iced tea**
1 teaspoon ground cinnamon
½ teaspoon ground cloves

Combine beverage crystals, sugar, instant tea and spices. Store in tightly covered jar. Makes 2 cups mix.

For 1 serving, place 1 teaspoon mix into cup. Add ¾ cup boiling water. Stir until mix is dissolved.

For 1 quart, place ⅓ cup mix into heatproof pitcher or bowl. Add 1 quart boiling water. Stir until mix is dissolved. Serve with lemon wedges, if desired.

ICED RUSSIAN TEA: Dissolve 2 teaspoons mix in ¾ cup boiling water. Pour over ice cubes in tall glass.

NOTE: Use more or less mix per serving, if desired.

*Or use 1 tub TANG® Sugar Free Beverage Crystals and reduce sugar to ¼ cup.

**Or use lemon-flavored unsweetened instant tea, presweetened iced tea mix OR lemon-flavored sugar free iced tea mix.

![Kahlúa] BARBECUE SAUCE

Barbecue sauces (good, complex, tinkered-with, homemade ones) are full of secret ingredients. Like chili (another male specialty dish), almost anything can be used in barbecue sauce, as long as the amount is kept small enough not to overpower. A little of this and a little of that can add up to a lot of big flavor, which is, after all, what barbecue is all about. Here the special touch is a generous dollop of Kahlúa®, the coffee-based Mexican liqueur, which adds sweet gloss and a dark, toasted flavor to a sauce that ranks among the best.

¼ cup (1 small) grated onion
2 large cloves fresh garlic, pressed
¼ cup oil
¼ cup KAHLÚA®
1 (8 oz.) can tomato sauce
3 tablespoons lemon juice
1 tablespoon Worcestershire sauce
¾ teaspoon dry oregano, crushed
¾ teaspoon dry basil, crushed
¾ teaspoon chili powder
¾ teaspoon salt
¼ teaspoon liquid smoke

In a saucepan, cook onion and garlic in oil over moderate heat, just until onion is transparent. Add all remaining ingredients. Stir to blend. Simmer 3 or 4 minutes. Use as all-purpose barbecue/baking sauce.

MAKES ABOUT 2 CUPS.

CINCINNATI CHILI

In Cincinnati, dueling diner chains, one originally Greek and the other Bulgarian, have made a major industry out of serving a thin, sweet-spiced chili that clearly suits the Midwestern palate. If you're in a Texas state of mind, the stuff won't impress you much, but served in the traditional Cincinnati Five-Way (spaghetti topped with chili, beans, grated cheese and onions), it is a simple, hearty regional food at its best.

1½ pounds lean ground beef
2 cups chopped onions
2 large garlic cloves, minced
2 teaspoons chili powder
¼ teaspoon ground cinnamon
Dash ground cloves
4 cups V8® Vegetable Juice
2 cans (16 ounces *each*) kidney beans, drained
Hot cooked spaghetti

1. In 6-quart Dutch oven over medium heat, cook ground beef, onions and garlic until beef is browned and onions are tender, stirring to separate meat. Spoon off fat.

2. Stir in chili powder, cinnamon and ground cloves; cook 2 minutes. Stir in V8® Juice. Heat to boiling; reduce heat to low. Cover; simmer 30 minutes.

3. Stir in beans. Cover; simmer 15 minutes, stirring occasionally. Serve over spaghetti.

MAKES 8¾ CUPS OR 11 SERVINGS.

GILDING THE LILY: For more flavor, the chili powder can be increased by at least 50 percent. For more fire, Spicy V8® Vegetable Juice can be substituted for the regular kind. Two teaspoons of unsweetened cocoa powder, added with the chili powder, will cut the sweetness and add depth of flavor. Without beans, this makes a great chili dog topper.

TOFFEE BLANKET

This recipe is here mainly because of its wonderful title. Since toffee is a favorite of mine, the thought of something (almost *anything*) being *blanketed* with the sweet, smooth stuff sends shivers up and down my sweet tooth. Coffee isn't always in toffee, but here it adds just the right dark edge that makes the flavor of this particular "blanket" really stand out.

1¾ cups strong S&W® 100% Colombian Coffee
   (Regular or Decaffeinated)
1 cup firmly packed brown sugar
2 Tbsp cornstarch
2 Tbsp butter
2 tsp vanilla

Chill ¼ cup coffee. Combine brown sugar and remaining 1½ cups coffee in medium saucepan; stir over low heat until sugar melts. Blend cornstarch with chilled coffee; stir into hot coffee mixture, cooking and stirring until sauce boils and thickens. Remove from heat. Add butter and vanilla; stir until butter dissolves. Serve warm over pound cake or ice cream.

MAKES ABOUT 2 CUPS.

GILDING THE LILY: This dessert sauce can also be used as a dip for strawberries, pineapple chunks and apple wedges.

3

THE CEREAL AISLE

Many of the most enduring brands of cereal were created in a health food fervor at the turn of the century. Even now, Kellogg's Corn Flakes®, Wheatena® and Quaker® Oats serve as shorthand symbols for high-fiber, good-for-you eating. Turning these cereals into hi-cal treats has always been one of the most subversive—not to mention sales-boosting—aims of back-of-the-box recipe developers. Breakfast, after all, is merely one meal, but bars and cookies can be enjoyed all day long.

Most of these cereal-based recipes cannot be called lean; they appear to have been designed to sell the crunchy products in question to those people who prefer to start their day eating juicy sausages, butter-fried eggs and steaming cocoa. If this shoe fits you, you are advised to grab a box of cereal and get cooking. The firm, the fit and the swivel-hipped, on the other hand, should probably skip this chapter altogether.

CHERRY DOT COOKIES

Today no company on earth sells more cereal than Kellogg's®, though the firm's beginnings were far from auspicious. The founder was John Harvey Kellogg, the doctor at a Battle Creek, Michigan, sanitarium and a man with some unusual beliefs. A Seventh Day Adventist, he advocated celibacy and practiced a number of clearly useless, if not downright dangerous, therapies on his wealthy patients. Eventually his search for a hard-to-chew food (he thought the exercise was good for the teeth) led him in 1898 to create corn flakes. Sold exclusively through mail order, corn flakes only really flourished after 1906, when Dr. Kellogg's brother Will bought him out and began marketing the cereal vigorously. One promotion, "Wink Day," was designed to provide a free box of corn flakes to any woman who would wink at her grocer on a Wednesday. For years these easy cookies were called Cherry Winks, possibly inspired by Will's promotion, and though the name has been changed for trademark purposes, the cookies remain sweetly colorful (they're a Christmas tradition in many homes) and simple to prepare.

2¼ cups all-purpose flour
2 teaspoons baking powder
½ teaspoon salt
¾ cup margarine, softened
1 cup sugar
2 eggs
2 tablespoons skim milk
1 teaspoon vanilla
1 cup chopped nuts
1 cup finely cut pitted dates
⅓ cup finely chopped maraschino cherries
2⅔ cups KELLOGG'S CORN FLAKES® cereal,
    crushed to 1⅓ cups
15 maraschino cherries, cut into quarters

1. Stir together flour, baking powder and salt. Set aside.

2. In large mixing bowl, beat margarine and sugar until light and fluffy. Add eggs. Beat well. Stir in milk and vanilla. Add flour mixture. Mix well. Stir in nuts, dates and the ⅓ cup chopped cherries.

3. Shape level measuring-tablespoons of dough into balls. Roll in KELLOGG'S CORN FLAKES® cereal. Place on baking sheets coated with cooking spray. Top each cookie with cherry quarter.

4. Bake at 350°F about 12 minutes or until lightly browned.

YIELD: 5 DOZEN, 2-INCHES IN DIAMETER.

WHEATENA® CHOCOLATE CHIP COOKIES

Fiber has become a kind of magic talisman, the culinary equivalent of the crucifix, keeping the vampires of fat and cholesterol at bay. Fiber has also come to represent something good for you but otherwise tasteless, to be gotten down but not enjoyed, the necessary payment for the pleasure of medium-rare steaks, cheese enchiladas and butter pecan ice cream. How nice, then, to report that Wheatena®, a hot, toasted wheat cereal that has been eaten for over one hundred years, is packed with fiber. Sure, you can eat a bowl at breakfast and feel virtuous (and if your diet is like mine, don't delay), but you can also stir Wheatena® into meat loaf, scalloped potatoes and, as this recipe shows, chocolate chip cookies, truly producing a treat that is as good for the rest of the body as it is for the mouth.

1¾ cups all-purpose flour
¾ cup WHEATENA®
1 teaspoon baking soda
¾ cup butter or margarine
¾ cup dark brown sugar, tightly packed
½ cup granulated sugar
1 egg
1 teaspoon vanilla
1 package (12 oz.) chocolate chips
1 cup chopped nuts (optional)

Preheat oven to 375°F. In small bowl combine flour, WHEATENA® and baking soda. In large bowl, beat butter and sugars until light and fluffy. Add egg and vanilla; beat until fluffy. Stir in flour mixture. Stir in chocolate chips and nuts. Drop by rounded teaspoonfuls onto ungreased cookie sheets. Bake approximately 10 to 12 minutes.

MAKES ABOUT 5 DOZEN 2½-INCH COOKIES.

CHOCOLATE SCOTCHEROOS

Seemingly alone among the endless spun-off cousins of Kellogg's® Rice Krispies Treats® (the fifty-plus-years-old back-of-the-box classic), this confection has achieved a status of its own. It's a slightly more complex recipe to make, but with their trio of candy bar flavors—chocolate, peanut butter and butterscotch—the bar cookies it produces are absolutely irresistible.

1 cup light corn syrup
1 cup sugar
1 cup peanut butter
6 cups KELLOGG'S® RICE KRISPIES® cereal
1 package (6 oz., 1 cup) semi-sweet chocolate
    morsels
1 package (6 oz., 1 cup) butterscotch morsels
Vegetable cooking spray

1. Measure corn syrup and sugar into large saucepan. Cook over medium heat, stirring frequently, until sugar dissolves and mixture begins to boil. Remove from heat. Stir in peanut butter. Mix well. Add KELLOGG'S® RICE CRISPIES® cereal. Stir until well coated. Press mixture into 13 × 9 × 2-inch pan coated with cooking spray. Set aside.

2. Melt chocolate and butterscotch morsels together in small saucepan over low heat, stirring constantly. Spread evenly over cereal mixture. Let stand until firm. Cut into 1 × 2-inch bars to serve.

YIELD: 48 BARS.

APPLE-GLAZED HAM LOAF

Though it comes from The Kellogg® Kitchens, this delicious loaf could just as well come from my mother's recipe file. She's made ham loaf for the family for years (mustard-, not apple-glazed), and her regular beef loaf always includes corn flakes, so this recipe seems merely an extension, a natural kitchen hybrid, one that automatically (to me, at least, and I'll wager to many others) tastes pretty much like home cooking is *supposed* to taste.

1 jar (10 oz.) apple jelly
¼ cup firmly packed brown sugar
3 tablespoons lemon juice
½ teaspoon dry mustard
2 eggs
3 cups KELLOGG'S CORN FLAKES® cereal, crushed to ¾ cup
¼ cup firmly packed brown sugar
¾ cup skim milk
⅓ cup finely chopped onion
⅛ teaspoon pepper
1 ½ teaspoons dry mustard
1 pound ground cooked ham
1 pound ground pork
Vegetable cooking spray

1. Preheat oven to 350°F. For glaze, stir together first four ingredients in small saucepan. Cook over low heat, stirring frequently, until jelly melts. Bring to a boil. Boil one minute, stirring constantly. Remove from heat. Cool to room temperature.

2. In large mixing bowl, beat eggs slightly. Add crushed cereal, the ¼ cup brown sugar, milk, onion, pepper and the 1½ teaspoons dry mustard. Beat well. Add ham and pork. Mix until combined. Shape into loaf. Place in pan coated with cooking spray or foil-lined shallow pan.

3. Bake about 1 hour and 15 minutes or until well browned. Brush loaf with glaze several times during last 30 minutes of baking. Serve with remaining glaze.

YIELD: 1 LOAF, 12 SLICES.

SCALLOPED CORN

My family's Midwestern roots meant plenty of corn on the table, and when I was growing up, it was, after potatoes, my favorite vegetable. Creamed corn often served as gravy over mashed spuds, corn on the cob was a frequent summertime treat and a corn flake–topped scalloped corn casserole, very much like this one, frequently showed up on holiday menus and at other big family gatherings. I always saved some to eat later, cold, and I always headed for the kitchen to scrape the sweet brown crust from the baking dish before it got washed.

1 can (12 oz.) cream-style corn
1 package (10 oz.) frozen corn, thawed
1 egg, well-beaten
⅔ cup skim milk
¼ teaspoon salt
½ teaspoon dry mustard
¼ teaspoon paprika
⅓ cup chopped green pepper
3 cups KELLOGG'S CORN FLAKES® cereal,
    crushed to 1½ cups
2 tablespoons margarine, melted
Vegetable cooking spray

1. Preheat oven to 350°F.

2. Combine cream-style corn, thawed corn, egg, milk, salt, mustard, paprika, green pepper, and ½ cup crushed cereal. Pour into 10 × 6 × 2-inch (1½ quart) glass baking dish lightly coated with cooking spray. Combine remaining cereal with margarine. Sprinkle over top. Bake 35 to 40 minutes or until set.

YIELD: 8 SERVINGS

GILDING THE LILY: I prefer roasted red pepper, fresh or from a jar, to the raw green called for. I have also augmented this casserole with some finely chopped pickled jalapeño peppers and a sliced green onion or two, which makes it delicious with a hickory- or mesquite-grilled steak.

ORIGINAL CRISPIX® MIX

The folks at Ralston-Purina, creators of Traditional Chex Party Mix, jealously guard their invention, understandable if for no other reason than that it's so easy to improvise upon and/or knock off entirely. One of my grandmothers made tons of something similar come holiday time (hers included Cheerios as I recall, so it could hardly have come from Ralston Purina), and I myself have published a Southwestern version, fired up with chili powder and other Tex-Mex touches. Kellogg's®, too, has put their spin on the genre, using Crispix®, their crisp waffle cereal first introduced in 1983, and it is a model modification of its kind.

7 cups KELLOGG'S® CRISPIX® cereal
1 cup mixed nuts
1 cup pretzels
3 tablespoons margarine, melted
¼ teaspoon garlic salt
¼ teaspoon onion salt
2 teaspoons lemon juice
4 teaspoons Worcestershire sauce

1. Combine KELLOGG'S® CRISPIX® cereal, nuts and pretzels in 13 × 9 × 2-inch baking pan. Set aside.

2. Stir together remaining ingredients. Gently stir spices and margarine into cereal mixture until evenly coated.

3. Bake at 250°F about 45 minutes, stirring every 15 minutes. Spread on paper towels to cool. Store in airtight container.

YIELD: 9 CUPS.

ORIENTAL CASHEW CRUNCH

Continuing a theme of adapting some other corporation's successful back-of-the-box notion in order to sell more of your own competing product, here's a party mix-type recipe with a fairly unusual Oriental twist, complete down to the chow mein noodles. Perhaps it's time to mix up a batch of several of these crunchy clones and conduct a tasting, to determine America's favorite variation.

One 16-ounce package Original QUAKER® Oat
    Squares Cereal (8 cups)
One 3-ounce can chow mein noodles (1½ cups)
1 cup cashews or peanuts
⅓ cup vegetable oil
3 tablespoons soy sauce
1 teaspoon garlic powder
1 teaspoon onion powder

1. Heat oven to 250°F. Combine first 3 ingredients in 13" × 9" pan; set aside.

2. Combine remaining 4 ingredients in small bowl; quickly pour over cereal mixture. Stir to coat evenly.

3. Bake 1 hour, stirring every 20 minutes; cool.

MAKES 10 CUPS.

GILDING THE LILY: Perhaps this would be good with a teaspoon or so of ground ginger added to the soy sauce mix.

CLASSIC HERB CHICKEN

For years, in the days when health foods had a wacky aura, wheat germ as much as anything symbolized the nutritional fringe. It's a measure of our increased knowledge of food that the crunchy stuff—the nutrient-packed heart of the wheat kernel—has joined the mainstream in a big way. Now found in the cereal aisle of most supermarkets, wheat germ is used as an add-on or sprinkle-over, not eaten as is, and few would consider it wacky. Here it adds a crisp coating to low-fat, oven-baked chicken.

1 cup KRETSCHMER® Wheat Germ
1 tablespoon Italian seasoning
2 treaspoons dried parsley
2 teaspoons dried minced onion
1 teaspoon garlic powder
¼ teaspoon salt (optional)
¼ teaspoon black pepper
½ cup water
1 egg white
2 split and skinned chicken breasts or one 2½ to 3 pound chicken, cut up and skinned

Heat oven to 400°F. Combine wheat germ and seasonings; set aside. Combine water and egg white. Dip chicken into egg white mixture, and then into wheat germ mixture, coating chicken thoroughly. Place in 13 × 9-inch baking pan; spray each chicken breast about 3 seconds with no-stick cooking spray. Bake 45 minutes or until tender and golden brown.

4 SERVINGS.

4

THE CANDY JAR

Candy should be enough, and usually it is. On-the-go Americans, desperately seeking snacks that can be eaten on the run and perennially shy of the next energy boost, mostly grab up their candy bars, caramels and other sweet treats and keep on moving. All well and good, unless you're the staff of a corporate test kitchen dedicated to the idea that eating the product for its own sake, in its original state, is, somehow, leaving a promise unfulfilled. ("A Milky Way® Bar is a terrible thing to waste.") And so we bring you this chapter, dedicated to the twin ideals that candy is really only a single ingredient in a larger, sweeter, richer and even more deliciously gooey candy-like something or other, and that you should go make a batch right now.

CREAMY MILKY WAY® BAR PUDDING

The best way, no doubt, to enjoy a Milky Way® Bar is just to unwrap it and get chewing. Still, it's worth knowing that when melted and then otherwise stirred, folded, drizzled or whipped, Milky Way® Bars can be turned into any number of rather posh sweets. You might offer candy bars as dessert only to the members of a visiting Little League team, but this chocolate pudding, topped with the chocolate sauce that follows, turns Milky Way® Bars into a dessert fit for company.

2 MILKY WAY® Bars (2.23 oz. ea.), sliced
¾ cup milk
2 tablespoons unsweetened cocoa
1 pkg. (4 servings size) vanilla flavored instant pudding and pie filling mix
1 container (8 oz.) sour cream

Stir MILKY WAY® Bars, ¼ cup milk and cocoa in medium saucepan over low heat until smooth.

Place mixture in medium bowl and chill 10 minutes or until cold. Stir in remaining milk and pudding mix. Blend with a wire whisk or rotary eater until smooth and slightly thickened. Blend in sour cream. Chill at least 30 minutes.

MAKES ABOUT 4 SERVINGS.

PREPARATION TIME: About 20 minutes

CHILLING TIME: 30 minutes

CHOCOLATE DESSERT SAUCE
4 MILKY WAY® Bars (2.23 oz. ea.), sliced
½ cup water

Stir MILKY WAY® Bars and water over low heat in small saucepan until smooth. Cool slightly and serve warm. Store any leftovers in the refrigerator, reheating the sauce when used again.

MAKES ABOUT 1½ CUPS.

CHOCOLATE CARAMEL NUT BARS

Here's a recipe that definitely should have appeared in my first back-of-the-box book. These nutty, multilayer caramel-chocolate bar cookies have legions of fans. Good any time, they're an especially fine Halloween giveaway, and they go well in a tin of Christmas cookies.

48 KRAFT® Caramels
1 can (5 ounces) evaporated milk, divided
1 package (2-layer size) German chocolate cake mix with pudding
½ cup (1 stick) PARKAY® Margarine, melted
1 cup BAKER'S® Semi-Sweet Real Chocolate Chips
1½ cups chopped walnuts, divided

Heat oven to 350°F.

Melt caramels with ⅓ cup of the milk in heavy saucepan over low heat, stirring frequently until smooth. Set aside.

Mix remaining milk, cake mix and margarine in large bowl. Press ½ of the cake mixture onto bottom of ungreased 13 × 9-inch baking pan. Bake 8 minutes.

Sprinkle chips and 1 cup of the walnuts over crust; top with caramel mixture, spreading to edges of pan. Top with teaspoonfuls of remaining cake mixture; press gently into caramel mixture. Sprinkle with remaining ½ cup walnuts.

Bake 18 minutes. Cool; cut into bars.

MAKES 24.

EASY GRASSHOPPER PIE

Sometimes we back-of-the-box detectives have to set aside our personal inclinations and write about foods we would rather not. In the case of grasshopper pie, a confection that I have always thought looked and tasted as though made of Crest toothpaste, I am honest and thorough and dedicated enough to acknowledge that millions of folks love the stuff and would probably be thrilled to see an easy recipe for making it. So, duty done, here it is. Enjoy . . . Now can I go home?

CRUST
2 cups (24) crushed chocolate sandwich cookies
¼ cup (½ stick) PARKAY® Margarine, melted

FILLING
1 package (10½ ounces) KRAFT® Miniature Marshmallows
¼ cup green creme de menthe
2 cups whipping cream, whipped

Crust: Mix crumbs and margarine. Press mixture onto bottom and sides of 9-inch pie plate. Refrigerate.

Filling: Microwave marshmallows and creme de menthe in large microwave-safe bowl on HIGH 1 to 2 minutes or until smooth when stirred, stirring every minute. Refrigerate 20 minutes or until slightly thickened.

Fold in whipped cream; spoon into crust. Freeze 4 to 6 hours or until firm. Garnish with jelly beans and coconut.

MAKES 8 SERVINGS.

CONVENTIONAL: Prepare crust as directed. Melt marshmallows with creme de menthe in large saucepan over low heat, stirring until smooth. Transfer to mixing bowl; refrigerate 20 minutes or until slightly thickened. Continue as directed.

VARIATIONS: Substitute ¼ cup milk for creme de menthe. Add a few drops each peppermint extract and green food coloring to filling mixture.

Substitute 1 prepared chocolate flavor crumb crust (6 ounces) for cookies and margarine.

TOFFEE FANTASY PIE

The Heath® Bar, a slim wafer of tender-but-crunchy almond toffee coated with chocolate, originated in 1919 at a small, family-owned confectionery business in Robinson, Illinois. In the following years the Heath family manufactured everything from butter to ice cream to Pepsi-Cola, but the overwhelming success of the toffee bar eventually convinced the family to specialize. Now owned by Leaf®, Incorporated, Heath® still produces only the classic bar, Heath® Bits (chopped-up bar, many tons of which get stirred into Ben and Jerry's Heath® Bar Crunch Ice Cream) and Bits 'O Brickle® (almond-toffee chips). As with most successful candy bars, the lion's share of the product is consumed as is, but unlike many candy bars, Heath's® simple, classic flavor lends itself to many other dessert preparations.

1½ cups milk
1 (3½-oz) pkg. instant vanilla pudding
1 (6-oz) pkg. HEATH® Bits
1 (8-oz) container non-dairy whipped topping, thawed
1 9-inch prepared pie shell, baked

Place milk and instant pudding in large bowl. Beat with wire whip until well blended, about one minute. Let stand five minutes.

Remove ¼ cup of HEATH® Bits and set aside. Gently fold the remaining crushed toffee bars and whipped topping into pudding. Pour mixture into baked and cooled pie shell. Sprinkle reserved crushed toffee bars on top for garnish.

Freeze at least six hours. Remove from freezer and let stand 10 minutes to soften before serving.

MAKES 8-10 SERVINGS.

CHERRY COFFEE CAKE

In the 1970s Heath® bought The Fenn Brothers, a Sioux Falls, South Dakota, candy company. In the process they acquired the rights to that firm's legendary Butter Brickle ice cream. (Brickle is a Scottish word for brittle and is presumably the source of the name for the Fenns' nougat ice cream flavoring bits.) The alliance was a logical one and eventually resulted in the marketing of Heath Bits 'O Brickle®, the almond-toffee chips that, if you can locate them, exceed almost any other baking chip the mind can conjure. Of course they make great cookies (bake a basic chipper recipe and substitute them for some or all of the chocolate called for), but if you'd like to enjoy your brickle at breakfast, try this sweet and sumptuous (but easy) treat.

1 2-layer-size package white cake mix
2 6-ounce packages (2 cups) HEATH Bits 'O Brickle®
1 21-ounce can cherry pie filling
½ cup all-purpose flour
½ cup packed brown sugar
½ teaspoon ground cinnamon
¼ cup margarine or butter
½ cup slivered almonds
1 cup sifted powdered sugar
4 to 5 teaspoons water

Prepare cake mix according to package directions. Stir in 1 package of the HEATH Bits 'O Brickle®. Grease and lightly flour a 13×9×2-inch baking pan. Spread batter evenly into the prepared pan. Spoon pie filling carefully over batter.

In a medium mixing bowl combine the flour, brown sugar and cinnamon. Cut in margarine or butter until mixture resembles coarse crumbs. Stir in the remaining package of the HEATH Bits 'O Brickle® and the almonds. Sprinkle on top of pie filling.

Bake in a 350°F oven for 40 to 45 minutes or until top is golden brown. In a small mixing bowl stir together the powdered sugar and water. Drizzle over warm coffee cake. Serve warm.

MAKES 20 SERVINGS.

GILDING THE LILY: I haven't tried it, but I can't shake the notion that this would be perfectly delicious prepared with peach pie filling.

CARAMELCORN

With commercial versions of this sweet, crunchy treat so ubiquitous, the only reason for making your own at home is that it is incomparably fresher and more delicious when warm. If during munching some of the sticky stuff becomes attached to the fingers of you and/or your little helpers, permission for licking is hereby granted.

28 KRAFT® Caramels
2 tablespoons water
2½ quarts popped corn

Heat oven to 250°F.

Mix caramels and water in 2-cup measure or medium bowl. Microwave on HIGH 1½ minutes.

Continue microwaving on HIGH 30 seconds to 1 minute or until sauce is smooth, stirring every 30 seconds.

Pour immediately over popped corn; toss until well coated. Spread onto greased cookie sheet to form single layer.

Bake 20 to 25 minutes; break apart.

MAKES 2½ QUARTS.

CONVENTIONAL: Melt caramels with water in saucepan over low heat, stirring until smooth. Continue as directed.

BUTTERFINGER™ COOKIES

Butterfinger™ candy bars, filled with a crunchy peanut butter honeycomb and coated with chocolate, are a secret and intensely enjoyed sweet snack for many. Hoarded in bedside nightstands and nibbled at midnight or bought on the way to work, tucked away in purse or pocket and consumed on the way home, as the antidote to one rotten day or another, Butterfingers™ hold a real—though private—sway over many people (Bart Simpson, you are not alone). For more public pleasure, please consider this recipe, a real find passed along by one of my spies at Nestlé®. It is made with so-called Butterfinger™ Chips, actually bite-sized mini-bars (frighteningly consumable—if they're not available in your area, be glad).

¾ cup sugar
½ cup butter or margarine, softened
1 egg
1¾ cups all-purpose flour
¾ teaspoon baking soda
¼ teaspoon salt
1 package (8 ounces) BUTTERFINGER™ Chips,
  coarsely chopped

Preheat oven to 375°F. In large mixer bowl beat sugar and butter until creamy. Beat in egg until light and fluffy. Blend in flour, baking soda and salt. Stir in chopped BUTTERFINGER™ Chips. Drop dough by rounded measuring tablespoonfuls onto ungreased cookie sheet.

Bake 11 to 13 minutes or until cookies are lightly browned. Let stand on cookie sheet 2 minutes. Cool on wire rack.

MAKES ABOUT 30 COOKIES.

5

BEANS, GRAINS AND PASTA

Image is everything, and these lowly carbohydrates are clearly working with a new PR firm. Often dismissed as peasant food, frequently blamed for intestinal discomfort and long thought of as fattening, beans, grains and pasta have undergone a rehabilitation that would awe even that fine American statesman Richard Nixon. I can remember a fairly recent time when struggling to be slim and fit meant ordering the waiter to remove the bread basket from the table. Beans appeared in punch lines more often than they did in menus, grains were eaten (if at all) for breakfast and spaghetti merely provided a bed for the meatballs. Now peasant food is what we *want* to eat, and starches are chic, not only turning up with a vengeance as glorious side dishes, but even starring as the main course on the plate. Zapped with herbs, garlic and chilies, laved with green-gold olive oil and sometimes even meatless (brave new world!), these high-style carbos have a host of less flashy, but no less tasty, cousins right on the back of the box. Read on.

LAYERED BEAN DIP

This party-time dish is a kind of back-of-the-box bonanza. Since it contains several staple ingredients, it's been adopted by any number of corporations. Makers of cheese, beans, salsa, sour cream, corn chips, chili and even chicken broth granules have published their take on (generically speaking) the Southwestern Layered Dip and Scoop Thing, and since it's utterly easy to assemble and addictively good to eat (also portable), somewhere out there tonight an estimated 1,332,406 people, at their own house or someone else's, are digging into one version or another. Here is the recipe from Old El Paso®, a nearly perfect example of its kind.

2 cans (16 ounces, each) OLD EL PASO® Refried Beans
1 can (4 ounces) OLD EL PASO® Chopped Green Chilies, drained
1 envelope (1¼ ounces) OLD EL PASO® Taco Seasoning Mix
2 ripe avocados, peeled and pitted
2 tablespoons lemon juice
1 jar (16 ounces) OLD EL PASO® Taco Sauce, mild, medium or hot, divided usage
1½ cups sour cream
3 cups shredded lettuce
1½ cups (6 ounces) shredded Cheddar cheese
Black olive slices
OLD EL PASO NACHIPS® Tortilla Chips

In medium bowl, mix together refried beans, green chilies and taco seasoning mix. Spread on a 12-inch round serving platter. Blend avocados, lemon juice and ½ cup taco sauce until smooth. Spread on top of bean mixture. Spread sour cream on top of avocado mixture. Top with shredded lettuce, cheese, taco sauce and olive slices. Serve with NACHIPS® Tortilla Chips.

8-10 SERVINGS.

GILDING THE LILY: When preparing this for serving at home, you may wish to warm the bean mixture (this works nicely in a microwave oven) before spreading it on the plate. If all other ingredients are at hand, the dip can be quickly assembled and served while the beans are still warm, which improves the flavor considerably. If you like cilantro, add about ½ cup, finely chopped, to the avocado mixture before spreading.

SPAGHETTI CASSEROLE

Why are Americans so absolutely taken by Italian cooking? Theories abound, ranging from soldiers returning from Italy after World War II with an indelible craving for the cuisine, to the disturbingly comfortable similarities between pizza and ketchup-doused cheeseburgers. Another reason (less bandied about but possibly more valid) is the missionary work undertaken by Italian-born chef Hector Boiardi. In 1938 Boiardi, a successful Cleveland restaurateur already famous for his spaghetti sauce, closed his eatery to devote himself full time to the manufacture of Italian food products. His complete dinners (now phonetically labeled Boyardee) revolutionized "cooking Italian," a process that was once, to Americans at least, mysterious, but that now seems almost second nature. So, yes, Virginia, there really was a Chef Boyardee, and though he died in 1985, his likeness still appears on every label.

1 package (19.5 oz.) CHEF BOYARDEE® Complete Dinner with Meat Sauce
1 package (10 oz.) frozen mixed vegetables, thawed
¾ cup dairy sour cream
½ cup chopped onion
½ cup shredded Cheddar cheese

Break spaghetti into small pieces and cook according to package directions; drain. Combine cooked pasta with sauce and grated cheese from package, vegetables, sour cream and onion. Pour mixture into a greased 2-quart casserole; sprinkle with Cheddar cheese. Bake in a 350°F oven for 25 to 30 minutes or until heated through.

SERVES 4 TO 6.

EASY LASAGNE

The Ronzoni® Macaroni Co. was founded in New York City in 1915 by Italian immigrant Emanuele Ronzoni. When the company was finally sold in 1984, it was the largest family-owned pasta company in the country and had for years been one of New York's favorite brands. Ronzoni® is now one of nine regional pasta companies owned by Hershey®, which recently closed the Queens, New York, Ronzoni® plant and moved its operation to northwestern Virginia, ending the manufacture, if not the cooking, of Ronzoni® pasta in Manhattan. This rather outrageous recipe (it's certainly not Italian) aroused a lot of consumer attention when first published, since it eliminates the pasta-boiled-in-water step, which not only shortens prep time for this popular family supper, but dirties one less pan as well.

2½ cups spaghetti sauce
1 cup water
8 oz. (9 pieces) RONZONI® Lasagne, uncooked
1¾ cups (15 oz.) ricotta cheese
3 cups (12 oz.) shredded mozzarella cheese, divided
¼ cup grated Parmesan cheese
2 tablespoons chopped fresh parsley
½ teaspoon salt
¼ teaspoon ground black pepper

Heat oven to 375°F. In medium saucepan, combine spaghetti sauce and water; heat to boiling, stirring frequently. Reduce heat; keep warm. In large bowl, stir together ricotta cheese, 2 cups mozzarella cheese, Parmesan cheese, parsley, salt and pepper. Pour ¾ cup sauce on bottom of 13×9×2-inch glass baking dish; arrange 3 pieces uncooked pasta lengthwise over sauce. Pour ½ cup sauce over pasta; spread with half of cheese mixture. Cover with ½ cup sauce. Repeat layers of pasta, sauce, cheese mixture and sauce. Top with remaining pasta and sauce; sprinkle with additional Parmesan cheese, if desired. Cover with foil; bake 60 minutes or until hot and bubbly. Sprinkle with remaining 1 cup mozzarella cheese. Let stand 10 minutes before cutting.

8 SERVINGS.

GILDING THE LILY: To avoid any hard, uncooked pasta edges, be certain all the lasagne pieces are moistened thoroughly by the sauce.

RONZONI

FETTUCCINE WITH ALFREDO SAUCE

Inspired by the creamy pasta tossed with a golden fork at Alfredo's of Rome (which is a pretty tony source for a back-of-the-box recipe), this formula, from Ronzoni®, isn't particularly old, and unless you've eaten it in Rome it's not likely to inspire nostalgia, but otherwise it's a perfect example of its type—quick, easy, delicious, foolproof. This is a first-course pasta; follow it with plain roast chicken or veal or an unsauced seafood entree.

½ pkg. (6 oz.) RONZONI® Fettuccine, uncooked
¼ cup butter or margarine
¾ cup grated Parmesan cheese
½ cup whipping cream
2 tablespoons chopped fresh parsley

Cook pasta according to package directions; drain. Meanwhile, in small saucepan, melt butter over medium heat; gradually stir in cheese, then cream, until well blended. Continue heating sauce, stirring constantly, just to boiling point. Remove from heat; stir in parsley. Toss sauce with hot pasta.

3 SERVINGS.

GILDING THE LILY: The recipe can be doubled, since it's a good company dish, and you're likely to have more than three diners anyway. With so few ingredients, use only the best, which in this case means real, imported Italian Parmigiano-Reggiano cheese.

BROCCOLI 'N RICE CASSEROLE

There ought to be some kind of hall of fame for back-of-the-package recipes that use five or more brand-name products. This one would qualify, even though two of the products (canned soup and french-fried onions) are made by other companies. At this rate of consumption, there's nothing wrong with spreading some of the business around. Now that the country has a President who says he likes broccoli (though I have yet to see him eat any), can we expect to have this served at the White House?

2 packages (10 ounces each) BIRDS EYE®
   Chopped Broccoli, thawed, drained
1½ cups cooked MINUTE® Rice
1 can (10¾ ounces) condensed cream of mushroom soup
1 jar (8 ounces) CHEEZ WHIZ® pasteurized Process Cheese Spread
1 can (2.8 ounces) French fried onions

Heat oven to 350°F.

In large bowl mix broccoli, rice, soup, process cheese spread and 1 cup onions until well blended. Spoon into 1½-quart casserole.

Bake 35 minutes.

Top with remaining onions; continue baking 5 minutes.

MAKES 8 TO 10 SERVINGS.

HUSH PUPPIES

I don't know how hush puppies actually got their name (I think they're too tasty to be thrown to the hungry dogs hanging around a Southern fish fry in order to keep them quiet, which is the usual story), but I do know that they're one of the easier and more delicious ways to get one of your daily carbohydrate food group servings. Team them with fried catfish by all means, or use them to accompany ham and eggs or a bowl of chili, and far from silencing your family, you'll elicit sighs of satisfaction. Here is a good basic recipe from Aunt Jemima®, which uses white cornmeal, preferred in the South.

Vegetable oil
1½ cups AUNT JEMIMA® Enriched White Corn Meal
½ cup all-purpose flour
2 tablespoons baking powder
1 teaspoon salt (optional)
¾ cup milk
½ cup finely chopped onion
1 egg, beaten

Heat 2-inch deep oil to 375°F. Combine remaining ingredients; mix well. Drop by rounded teaspoonfuls into hot oil, frying a few at a time until golden brown. Drain on paper towels.

4 TO 6 SERVINGS.

GILDING THE LILY: Yellow cornmeal can be substituted. Chopped roasted red pepper or minced pickled jalapeño peppers can be substituted for some of the onion. Green onions can replace the white onions.

OLD FASHIONED RICE PUDDING

Genuine rice puddings (no instant boxed mixes permitted) fall into two general categories—stirred and baked. Prepared from scratch with eggs, milk, sugar, plenty of vanilla, either version is one of the simpler, sweeter, happier treats a cook can make. The stirred, stovetop approach results in a looser, creamier pudding, while the baked method yields something a little firmer, more like a set custard. Uncle Ben's®, the Houston-based rice company, quite naturally has recipes for both, but space limitations (and a touch of the missionary) compel me to print only my favorite.

1¾ cups water
½ cup UNCLE BEN'S® CONVERTED® Brand Rice
½ teaspoon salt
2 cups milk
2 eggs, beaten
⅓ cup sugar
1 teaspoon vanilla
¼ cup raisins, steamed in water and drained (optional)
Nutmeg or Cinnamon (optional)

Bring water to a boil. Stir in rice and salt. Cover and simmer until all water is absorbed, about 30 minutes. Add milk and boil gently, stirring occasionally, until mixture thickens slightly, about 5 minutes. Combine eggs, sugar and vanilla in a bowl. Gradually stir in rice mixture; mix well. Pour into greased 1½-quart casserole. If desired, stir in raisins and sprinkle nutmeg or cinnamon over top. Place casserole in pan containing about 1 inch hot water. Bake, uncovered, in 350°F oven for 45 to 50 minutes, or until knife inserted near center comes out clean.

MAKES 5 TO 6 SERVINGS.

GILDING THE LILY: If you find dried cherries, either tart or sweet, they make a fine substitution for the raisins (plump them in warm water). Serve the pudding barely warm, topped with a dollop of whipped cream, for family or company dessert; enjoy any leftovers cold and plain, as a midnight snack or a wonderful breakfast.

WILD RICE CHICKEN SUPREME

Not a grain, but a grass seed, wild rice for years was exclusively hand-harvested in the wild, a state of affairs that rendered it both rare and expensive. Now largely cultivated and harvested by specially designed combines, wild rice—even a small amount of it—packs a lot of cachet, which means Uncle Ben's packaged blend of Converted® Long Grain & Wild Rice seems the height of elegance, starchwise, to many. This time-tested recipe for turning a boxed side dish into a satisfying main dish casserole sometimes disappears from the Uncle Ben's® box, always drawing complaints from those who miss its tasty convenience.

1 package (6 ounces) UNCLE BEN'S® Long
   Grain & Wild Rice Original Recipe
¼ cup butter or margarine
⅓ cup chopped onion
⅓ cup flour
1 teaspoon salt
Dash black pepper
1 cup half & half
1 cup chicken broth
2 cups cubed cooked chicken
⅓ cup diced pimiento
⅓ cup chopped fresh parsley
¼ cup chopped slivered almonds

Cook contents of one 6-ounce package UNCLE BEN'S® Long Grain & Wild Rice as directed on package. While rice is cooking, melt butter in large saucepan. Add onion and cook over low heat until tender. Stir in flour, salt and pepper. Gradually stir in half & half and chicken broth. Cook, stirring constantly, until thickened. Stir in chicken, pimiento, parsley, almonds and cooked rice. Pour into a greased 2-quart casserole. Bake, uncovered, in 400°F oven for 30 minutes.

MAKES 6–8 SERVINGS.

GILDING THE LILY: The dish can also be prepared with turkey, either leftover holiday bird or smoked turkey breast.

CALIFORNIA BEAN BAKE

S&W® Fine Foods, located in San Ramon, California, is a packer of premium fruits and vegetables, among other foodstuffs. Founded in 1896 by Samuel Sussman and Gustav Wormser with the goal of uncompromising quality, S&W® remains unequaled in the industry. Though more widely available in the West, some of the products occasionally turn up further east. I learned years ago not to bother making chili without S&W's® dark red kidney beans (even though it always means a scavenger hunt through Manhattan's supermarkets), and indeed, beans and tomatoes account for much of the company's line, one extensive enough to also include olives, sauerkraut, spiced crabapples, tuna, cranberry sauce, brown bread (!) and coffee. The seasoned beans, in particular, are popular, as is this easy, classic baked bean casserole.

2 cans (16 ounces each) S&W® Brick Oven Baked Beans
2 cans (15½ ounces each) S&W® Texas Style Barbecue Beans
1 can (14½ ounces) S&W® Italian Style Stewed Tomatoes, undrained
3 slices bacon, crisply cooked and crumbled
1 can (2.8 ounces) french-fried onions

in a 2½-quart casserole, combine first four ingredients and half of the french-fried onions. Top with remaining french-fried onions. Bake, uncovered, at 350°F for 45 to 50 minutes, or until heated through and bubbly.

SERVES 6 TO 8.

LENTIL SOUP

Goya® Foods, Inc. is the largest privately owned Hispanic company in the country. Founded in 1936 in New York City's TriBeCa area, the business, whose owners are Basque, by way of Puerto Rico, has boomed. The line, which originally included only olives, olive oil and canned sardines, now boasts hundreds of items, covering not only Spanish and Caribbean specialties, but, increasingly, Mexican as well. In the dried and canned bean departments, few can equal Goya's® breadth and quality. Because beans are so internationally versatile, Goya's® promotional product recipes are not exclusively Hispanic, as this easy classic recipe proves.

1 cup GOYA® Dried Lentils
¼ pound smoked ham or sausage
1 small onion, minced
1 stalk celery, diced
1 clove garlic
1 cube GOYA® Chicken or Beef Bouillon
6 cups water

Rinse lentils. Combine all ingredients in a medium saucepan. Bring to a boil, then simmer until tender (about 2 hours). Salt and pepper to taste. For a soup with an Italian flair, simmer with 1 cup canned tomatoes and add Parmesan cheese.

REFRIED BLACK BEANS

Among the "in" beans, none are inner than black ones. As tout le monde has made black the fashionable color to wear, so have the tastemakers crowned the black bean the chic-est to eat. One way to get raves automatically is to substitute black beans for any other bean in almost any bean dish. Here, by way of example, is a bravo-earning recipe from Goya®, one that is quick, easy and rich.

1 16 oz. can GOYA® Black Beans, drained and rinsed
4 tablespoons GOYA® Olive Oil
2 slices bacon
1 clove garlic, crushed
1 medium onion, chopped fine
1 tomato, seeded and chopped
Salt & pepper to taste

1. Mash beans by hand, or puree in a blender or food processor.
2. Cook bacon until crisp; stir drippings into pureed beans. Discard bacon, or crush into bean mixture.
3. Sauté onion and garlic in 2 tablespoons oil; add tomato and simmer 2 minutes. Add small amount of bean mixture along with small amount more oil, and keep repeating until you have a rich creamy paste.
4. Serve as a side-dish, or with tacos or burritos.

SERVES 6.

GILDING THE LILY: This is also good with scrambled eggs and wonderful under the cheese on nachos, but it is unlikely that it can be stretched to feed six; double the recipe at least, or else trim the guest list.

6
PEANUT BUTTER AND JELLY

Like Rogers and Astaire, pink and charcoal gray, or baseball and spring, peanut butter and jelly are seemingly ordained natural partners, combining to create a powerful impression that is very much greater than the sum of its humble parts. Technically a trio, since Wonder bread or whatever brand you grew up tall and strong eating should also be given billing, PB&J sandwiches tap into some deep genetic material, immediately recognized and instantly welcome at the child's first sticky bite. We may grow out of the urge (or at least for the sake of our waistlines suppress it), but it's unlikely that this craving ever quite disappears from some shadowed storage place in the food section of our brains, and we're always susceptible. In the interests of keeping even childless grown-ups buying jar after jar, makers of both products have not relied totally on the power of deep-seated cravings, and so have looked to the back of the package, with the following intriguing results.

PASTA WITH PEANUT SAUCE

Authentic oriental sesame noodles are made with sesame paste, but over the years the convenient substitution of peanut butter has created a taste identity that is overwhelming, which leads to the inevitable conclusion that most people will find this dish of noodles, using the relatively new peanut butter from Reese's®, delicious.

1 package (16-oz.) Thin Spaghetti or Spaghetti, uncooked
½ cup REESE'S® Creamy or Crunchy Peanut Butter
¼ cup chopped green onion
2 tablespoons light soy sauce
1 clove garlic, minced
1 teaspoon finely chopped fresh ginger or ¾ teaspoon ground ginger
2 teaspoons hot pepper sauce
⅔ cup chicken broth
¼ cup peanut or vegetable oil
1 lb. cooked skinless chicken breasts, cut into 1-inch cubes
3 cups thin red pepper strips

Cook pasta according to package directions; drain. Meanwhile in large saucepan, stir together peanut butter, green onion, soy sauce, garlic, ginger and hot pepper sauce. Stir in broth until smooth. Slowly add oil, stirring constantly until well blended. Over medium heat cook until warm (do not boil). Stir in chicken and pepper strips. Toss hot pasta with warm sauce.

8 SERVINGS (ABOUT 1¾ CUPS EACH).

GILDING THE LILY: The dish is as rich as you would expect it to be and the suggested portion is an appetizer, not an entree. A tablespoon or two of fresh lime juice will enliven things considerably, and the dish is incomparably better with fresh ginger.

PEANUT BUTTER AND JELLY SWIRL BUNDT CAKE

If you can think of grape jelly and not think of peanut butter you must be a recent immigrant from a distant star system. Welch's® is the brand we earthlings reach for when we hunger for peanut butter and jelly. First manufactured in 1923 by a company originally founded to produce a nonalcoholic alternative to communion wine for teetotal Methodist churches, the jelly was eventually packed in decorated glasses (Tom and Jerry, the Flintstones and Howdy Doody come immediately to my mind), no doubt contributing to its kid appeal. No directions are needed for making a PB&J sandwich, but turning the concept into a Bundt cake requires the following formula.

2½ cups all-purpose flour
1½ teaspoons baking powder
1 teaspoon baking soda
½ teaspoon salt
½ cup unsalted butter, at room temperature
2 cups sugar
¼ cup chunky-style peanut butter
2 teaspoons vanilla extract
3 large eggs
1 cup dairy sour cream
½ cup WELCH'S® Grape Jelly

Preheat oven to 350°F. Place baking rack in bottom third of oven. Whisk together flour, baking powder, baking soda and salt; set aside. In large bowl of an electric mixer, beat butter and sugar together until light and fluffy. Add peanut butter and vanilla, beating until well combined. Add eggs, one at a time, beating until incorporated. Beat in sour cream. Reduce mixer to lowest speed and gradually add flour mixture, mixing until just blended.

Spoon half of the batter (about 3 cups) into a greased 12-cup Bundt pan. Dollop 3 tablespoons of the jelly over batter, avoiding edges of pan. Partially stir jelly into batter using a skewer or thin-bladed knife. Spoon remaining batter into pan and dollop and swirl remaining jelly into batter.

Bake for 1 hour or until a wooden pick inserted into center comes out clean. Let cake cool in pan for 10 minutes, then invert onto wire rack. Serve warm or at room temperature.

GILDING THE LILY: Though the recipe doesn't suggest it, a piece of this cake absolutely requires a big glass of ice-cold milk.

SOUTHERN JAM CAKE

Cakes flavored or filled with preserves date from a time when there were actually seasons, and fruit like strawberries or blueberries remained unavailable many months of the year. When bakers craved berries, they headed for the cellar and brought up a jar of home-bottled jam, turning the abundance and hard work of the past summer into a fall or winter treat. Southerners, perhaps even more so than dessert lovers from other regions, favor jam cakes. This recipe from Borden® is an excellent example of the genre and even more homey when slathered with the Maple Frosting below.

1 cup margarine or butter, softened
1 cup sugar
5 eggs
1 (16-ounce) jar BAMA® Blackberry Jam or
   Preserves
1 cup BAMA® Strawberry Preserves
3 cups unsifted flour
1 tablespoon baking soda
2 teaspoons ground allspice
2 teaspoons ground cinnamon
½ teaspoon ground cloves
1 cup BORDEN® Buttermilk
Maple Frosting*
Chopped nuts, optional

Preheat oven to 350°F. In large mixer bowl, beat margarine and sugar until fluffy. Add eggs, 1 at a time, beating well after each addition. Stir in jam and preserves. Stir together dry ingredients; add alternately with buttermilk to jam mixture. Turn into 3 well-greased wax paper–lined 9-inch layer cake pans. Bake 40 minutes or until wooden pick inserted near center comes out clean. Cool 5 minutes; remove from pans. Cool completely. Frost with Maple Frosting; garnish with nuts if desired.

*MAPLE FROSTING: In mixer bowl, beat 1 (8-ounce) package cream cheese until fluffy. Add 1½ pounds sifted confectioners' sugar (about 6 cups), 2 teaspoons maple flavoring and 1 teaspoon milk; mix well. Add additional milk, 1 teaspoon at a time, for desired consistency.

PEANUT BUTTER SAUCE

Peanut butter ice cream is good, but somehow peanut butter sauce over ice cream is even better. The following mini-recipes from Skippy® allow you to mix and match sauces and ice creams to create a veritable ice cream parlor.

½ cup SKIPPY® SUPER CHUNK® Peanut Butter
½ cup KARO® Light or Dark Corn Syrup
2 tablespoons milk

In small bowl stir together peanut butter, corn syrup and milk until well-blended. Serve over ice cream. Store in tightly covered container in refrigerator.

MAKES ABOUT 1 CUP.

CHOCOLATE PEANUT BUTTER SAUCE: Follow recipe for Peanut Butter Sauce. Omit milk. Add ½ cup chocolate-flavored syrup. Makes 1⅓ cups.

PEANUT BUTTER AND JELLY SAUCE: Follow recipe for Peanut Butter Sauce. Omit milk. Add ½ cup grape or strawberry jelly, melted. Makes about 1⅓ cups.

TOASTED COCONUT PINEAPPLE PEANUT BUTTER SAUCE: Follow recipe for Peanut Butter Sauce. Omit milk. Drain 1 can (8 oz.) crushed pineapple in own juice; reserve 3 tablespoons juice. Add pineapple, reserved juice and ½ cup toasted flaked coconut. Makes about 1½ cups.

GILDING THE LILY: Creative minds will also see these sauces as suitable for topping pancakes, waffles or fresh fruit. To toast coconut, spread it in a metal pan (like a cake tin) and bake at 375°F, stirring often, until golden brown, about 12 minutes.

MANHATTAN MEATBALLS

These tangy, savory and slightly smoky meatballs, swimming in barbecue sauce and apricot preserves, make great cocktail-time eating. To those without back-of-the-box experience and to those who did not grow up in the Fifties, such a chafing dish pairing of sweet and meat may seem odd, but rest assured, it's not. The proof is in the eating.

2 pounds lean ground beef
2 cups soft bread crumbs
½ cup chopped onion
2 eggs
2 tablespoons chopped fresh parsley
1 teaspoon salt
2 tablespoons PARKAY® Margarine
1 jar (10 ounces) KRAFT® Apricot Preserves
½ cup KRAFT® Barbecue Sauce

Mix meat, crumbs, onion, eggs, parsley and salt. Shape into 1-inch meatballs.

Heat oven to 350°F.

Brown meatballs in margarine in large skillet on medium heat; drain. Place in 13 × 9-inch baking dish.

Stir preserves and barbecue sauce together; pour over meatballs.

Bake 30 minutes, stirring occasionally.

MAKES 6 DOZEN.

VARIATIONS: Substitute 1 pound ground pork and 1 pound ground veal for ground beef.
    Substitute KRAFT® Thick 'N Spicy Original Barbecue Sauce for regular barbecue sauce.

GILDING THE LILY: Both suggested variations employed together will result in a far superior meatball. (The spicier, hotter barbecue sauce, in particular, will offset the sweetness of the preserves. You may even wish to fire things up further with the addition of some hot pepper sauce.) Serve them piping hot, in a chafing dish, with toothpicks and plenty of napkins.

7

DRESSINGS FOR DINNER

Perhaps when scientists finally locate that place where one can stand back and get a real good look at the universe, it will be found to be turning on a ball bearing glistening with mayonnaise. What did cooks do before the delicious lubrication of manufactured mayo? Well, they made it from scratch, but only during cool weather, and it was tricky and often broke, and there was a lot of swearing heard in the land and the food was, sad to say, dry. Now mayonnaise is a product, hurled into some kind of permanent suspension by great machines, and it and its bottled and powdered salad dressing cousins are spreading out to moisten the rest of the world, leaving untouched perhaps only the French, who persist in thinking of vinaigrettes and mayonnaise as delicate things, whisked up at the last minute with fresh ingredients, and who will never know the pleasures of the following.

SEVEN-LAYER SALAD

I first experienced this enduring do-ahead dish when visiting the salad bar of a restaurant in my home town in Colorado several years back. "What is *that*?" I asked the craggy gent in line ahead of me. "Looks like train wreck," he growled, spooning up a substantial serving. It did indeed, but it tasted wonderful, and I went back for seconds. There are many variations: this one from Kraft® includes tomatoes; others boast spinach and sliced black olives or crumbled blue cheese. All show up often at reunion picnics, church socials, potluck suppers and other bring-along meals.

6 cups shredded lettuce
2 cups chopped tomatoes
2 cups sliced mushrooms
1 package (10 ounces) BIRDS EYE® Green Peas, thawed, drained
4 ounces KRAFT® Mild Cheddar Cheese, cubed
1 cup red onion rings
2 cups MIRACLE WHIP® Light Salad Dressing

Layer lettuce, tomatoes, mushrooms, peas, cheese and onions in 2-quart serving bowl.

Spread salad dressing over onions, sealing to edge of bowl; cover.

Refrigerate several hours or overnight. Garnish with crisply cooked bacon slices, crumbled, and additional cheddar cheese, shredded, if desired.

MAKES 8 SERVINGS.

GILDING THE LILY: If you have buttermilk on hand (I always seem to), thin the dressing with a few spoonfuls.

FISH AU GRATIN

Bring Out The Best®

BLUE RIBBON®

HELLMANN'S REAL MAYONNAISE®

More mayo magic. A few tablespoons of the wonderful stuff, spread over a piece of fish and sprinkled with bread crumbs and Parmesan cheese, keeps the fish lusciously moist while baking into a satisfyingly crunchy crust. (Since fish cookery stumps even some fairly good cooks, a method this foolproof has great appeal.) An almost identical preparation for bluefish, in which the mayonnaise is spiked with a good bit of Dijon mustard, appears on the menu of one of Boston's best seafood restaurants.

3 tablespoons fine dry bread crumbs
3 tablespoons grated Parmesan cheese
Dash ground red pepper
¾ pound fish fillets, such as flounder or sole
3 tablespoons HELLMANN'S® or BEST FOODS®
 Real Mayonnaise

in shallow dish or on sheet of waxed paper, stir together crumbs, cheese and pepper. Brush all sides of fish fillets with real mayonnaise; coat with crumb mixture. Arrange in single layer in shallow baking pan so that fillets are just touching. Bake in 375°F oven 8 minutes or until golden and fish flakes easily. Makes 3 servings.

GILDING THE LILY: If you like the mustard idea, use about 1 tablespoon of good-quality Dijon mustard, replacing an equal amount of mayonnaise, or, for extra saucy fish, adding it on to the amount of mayo called for in the recipe.

78

AMAISIN RAISIN CAKE

The unexpected but undeniably successful moisture-producing magic of mayonnaise (think what it does for a dry turkey sandwich), which is, after all, mostly eggs and oil, is never more evident than in this apple-, nut- and raisin-studded spice cake. A Hellmann's®/Best Foods® favorite for years, it's an excellent keeper and will hold up for several days of family nibbling. The cake can also be garnished with whipped cream or hard sauce and served at teatime or as the delicious dessert for a company dinner, simply perfect on a crisp autumn night.

3 cups flour
2 teaspoons baking soda
1½ teaspoons cinnamon
½ teaspoon ground nutmeg
½ teaspoon salt
¼ teaspoon ground cloves
2 eggs
2 cups sugar
1 cup HELLMANN'S® or BEST FOODS® Real
  Mayonnaise
⅓ cup milk
3 cups coarsely chopped apples
1 cup raisins
1 cup coarsely chopped walnuts

Grease and flour 12-cup fluted tube pan. In medium bowl combine flour, baking soda, cinnamon, nutmeg, salt and cloves. In large bowl with mixer at high speed, beat together eggs and sugar 2 minutes or until light and fluffy. Reduce speed to low; beat in real mayonnaise until blended. Add flour mixture in 4 additions alternately with milk, beginning and ending with flour. (Batter will be thick.) Stir in apples, raisins and walnuts. Turn into prepared pan. Bake in 350°F oven 55 to 60 minutes or until toothpick inserted in center comes out clean. Cool in pan 10 minutes. Remove from pan; cool completely on wire rack.

MAKES 12 SERVINGS.

GILDING THE LILY: Buttermilk can be substituted for the regular milk. The apples are especially nice when left unpeeled. I prefer golden raisins and have also made the cake with sun-dried cherries. Pecans can be substituted for the walnuts.

SWEET 'N SPICY GLAZE

Among the zillions of back-of-the-box recipes that could not be included in my first collection, few had more vocal supporters than this easy, three-ingredient stir-up. Combining basic, nonperishable pantry items—the kind you're likely to have on hand anyway—and providing a sweetly oniony glaze for everything from chicken to frankfurters, it's simple, quick, easy to remember and it tastes good, too: quintessential back-of-the-package cookery.

1 envelope LIPTON® RECIPE SECRETS ™ Onion
  Recipe Soup Mix
1 jar (20 oz.) apricot preserves
1 cup (8 oz.) WISH-BONE® Sweet 'N Spicy
  French Dressing

In small bowl, blend all ingredients. Use as a glaze for chicken, spareribs, kabobs, hamburgers or frankfurters. Brush on during the last half of cooking. Can be stored covered in the refrigerator up to 2 weeks.

MAKES ABOUT 2½ CUPS GLAZE.

NOTE: Recipe can be doubled.

BUFFALO WINGS

There is some dispute (there always is when the food is good) about the creator of this unique snack, but pop historians generally credit Theresa Bellissimo, owner of the Anchor Bar in Buffalo, New York. Chicken wings (mostly fat and skin), deep-fried and dipped into creamy blue cheese dressing, won't win any nutrition awards (and almost nobody bothers with the celery accompaniment), but for zesty eating they can't be beat. Like most bar grub, Buffalo wings are fairly low cost, and this broiled variation, from the Lipton® Kitchens, even reduces the fat somewhat. Remember it, come next Super Bowl Sunday.

24 chicken wings (about 4 pounds)
1 envelope LIPTON® RECIPE SECRETS™ Golden
   Onion Recipe Soup Mix
½ cup IMPERIAL® Margarine, melted
2 tablespoons white vinegar
2 tablespoons water
2 cloves garlic
1½ to 2 teaspoons ground red pepper
1 teaspoon ground cumin
1 cup WISH-BONE® Chunky Blue Cheese
   Dressing

Cut tips off chicken wings (save tips for soup). Halve remaining chicken wings at joint.

In food processor or blender, process Golden Onion Recipe Soup Mix, margarine, vinegar, garlic, pepper and cumin until blended; set aside.

Broil chicken 12 minutes or until brown, turning after 6 minutes. Brush with ½ of the soup mixture, then broil 2 minutes or until crisp. Turn, then brush with remaining soup mixture and broil an additional minute. Serve with WISH-BONE® Chunky Blue Cheese Dressing and, if desired, celery sticks.

MAKES 24 WINGS.

GILDING THE LILY: It doesn't have anything to do with Buffalo, but offering some salsa as a dip along with the blue cheese dressing would give the low-calorie crowd something to cheer about.

PINE-APPLE COLESLAW

Making coleslaw, never one of the tougher kitchen chores, is even easier when Kraft's® prepared coleslaw dressing is used. Apple and pineapple add a pleasant sweetness, making the slaw a good accompaniment to ham and other smoked or salty meats.

3 cups shredded cabbage
1 can (8¼ ounces) crushed pineapple, drained
1 cup chopped apple
KRAFT® Coleslaw Dressing

Mix cabbage, pineapple, apple and enough dressing to moisten. Refrigerate.

MAKES 8 SERVINGS.

GILDING THE LILY: My experience with this recipe suggests that if you really want 8 servings, you will need to double or even triple the above proportions.

HONEY MUSTARD CHICKEN SANDWICHES

Dried salad dressing mixes have always struck me as useless for a couple of reasons. First, I can whisk up a classic vinaigrette with good vinegar, excellent olive oil, fresh garlic, imported mustard and an herb—dried or not—of choice in little more time than it takes to make the packaged dressing. Two, the packaged stuff tastes too strong, more than a little like a marinade. In fact, that is precisely why it works so well in this back-of-the-dressing-mix-packet recipe in which it is used as a marinade for grilled chicken. And who doesn't like sandwiches?

1 envelope GOOD SEASONS® Honey Mustard
 Salad Dressing Mix
⅓ cup orange juice or water
⅓ cup oil
3 boneless skinless chicken breasts, split
½ cup mayonnaise
6 sandwich buns, toasted
Lettuce
Tomato slices

Combine salad dressing mix, orange juice and oil in cruet or jar with tight-fitting lid; cover. Shake well. Reserve 2 tablespoons of the dressing. Pour remaining dressing over chicken in shallow dish or pan; cover. Refrigerate at least 3 hours or overnight to marinate.

Meanwhile, stir reserved dressing into mayonnaise; refrigerate until ready to use.

Broil chicken 4 inches from heat about 8 minutes; turn and baste. Broil 8 minutes longer or until cooked. Serve on sandwich buns with lettuce, tomato and honey mustard mayonnaise.

MAKES 6 SERVINGS.

GILDING THE LILY: The chicken breasts can also be cooked on a grill. For juicier chicken, shorten the cooking time by about 5 minutes.

ORIGINAL RANCH® DIP

I've always been confused about a flavor described as "ranch" that people actually *like*. ("Barnyard," after all, is no culinary compliment.) Somehow, in a triumph of marketing, we have come to associate ranch with a creamy, garlicky buttermilk flavor, livestock-free, and fortunately for the folks at HIDDEN VALLEY, we love it. Here's the recipe for an easy dip using the powdered RANCH® dressing mix, one that comes with a full array of interesting variations. Offer vegetables and/or chips for dunking.

2 cups (1 pint) sour cream
¼ cup mayonnaise
1 package (1 ounce) HIDDEN VALLEY RANCH®
  Milk Recipe Original Ranch® salad dressing
  mix

In medium bowl, whisk together all ingredients. Refrigerate at least 30 minutes before serving.

MAKES ABOUT 2½ CUPS.

VARIATIONS: Add any one of the following to prepared dip: 1 avocado, mashed, plus 1 teaspoon lemon juice and a dash of hot pepper sauce; ½ pared seeded cucumber, diced, plus ⅛ to ¼ teaspoon curry powder; ½ cup chopped shrimp or clams, plus 1 teaspoon lemon juice; 1 package (10 ounces) frozen spinach, thawed and squeezed dry, plus 1 tablespoon prepared mustard with horseradish.

8

FROM THE BAKER'S PANTRY

Ingredients for baking are among the most fundamental of processed foods. (Indeed, so elementary are butter, sugar and eggs that I have not even included them in this book.) There are few gimmicks here—most of these ingredients we don't even eat on their own (well, okay, chocolate chips), and they seem like a palette of oil paints, waiting to be transformed by the skill of the artist into something sweet and extraordinary. Most of the recipes in the baker's pantry are equally clean-lined, with only a few surprises, to show us the test kitchens haven't lost their ability to slip a secret ingredient in now and then. Among these home-baked cakes, brownies, bars, cookies and pies, there are just enough barbecue sauces, sweet and sour chicken stir-frys and molded coleslaw salads to make things *really* interesting.

DEEP DARK CHOCOLATE CAKE

The name pretty much describes it to a T, and every cook ought to have the recipe for such a cake in his or her files. I know there are those who swear by, and only bake, packaged cake mixes. Personally, while I like their texture, I think that most of them taste funny. But when a scratch cake is this moist, chocolaty and easy to assemble, there's no need to open a box of anything except powdered cocoa. This is one of Hershey's® most enduring recipes.

2 cups sugar
1¾ cups all-purpose flour
¾ cup HERSHEY'S® Cocoa or HERSHEY'S® European Style Cocoa
1½ teaspoons baking powder
1½ teaspoons baking soda
1 teaspoon salt
2 eggs
1 cup milk
½ cup vegetable oil
2 teaspoons vanilla extract
1 cup boiling water
One-Bowl Buttercream Frosting (recipe follows)

Heat oven to 350°F. Grease and flour two 9-inch round baking pans or one 13×9×2-inch baking pan. In large mixer bowl, stir together sugar, flour, cocoa, baking powder, baking soda and salt. Add eggs, milk, oil and vanilla; beat on medium speed of electric mixer 2 minutes. Remove from mixer; stir in boiling water (batter will be thin). Pour batter into prepared pans. Bake 30 to 35 minutes for round pans, 35 to 40 minutes for rectangular pan or until wooden pick inserted in center comes out clean. Cool 10 minutes; remove from pans to wire racks. Cool completely. (Cake may be left in rectangular pan, if desired.) Frost with One-Bowl Buttercream Frosting.

8 TO 10 SERVINGS.

ONE-BOWL BUTTERCREAM FROSTING
6 tablespoons butter or margarine, softened
2⅔ cups powdered sugar
½ cup HERSHEY'S® Cocoa or HERSHEY'S® European Style Cocoa
⅓ cup milk
1 teaspoon vanilla extract

In small mixer bowl, beat butter. Add powdered sugar and cocoa alternately with milk; beat to spreading consistency (additional milk may be needed). Blend in vanilla.

ABOUT 2 CUPS FROSTING.

GILDING THE LILY: Room-temperature buttermilk can be substituted for the regular milk in the frosting.

RED VELVET COCOA CAKE

A Depression-era recipe from Hershey®, Red Velvet Cocoa Cake (which originally called for vegetable shortening rather than butter) is far moister and more chocolaty than its modest amount of cocoa would lead you to believe. It's also rather *red*, thanks to the inclusion of a tablespoon of food coloring, meant, perhaps, to evoke classic Devil's Food, in which an excessive amount of baking soda causes the traditional reddish color. The cake can be frosted with One-Bowl Buttercream Frosting (page 86), but the vanilla-flavored recipe below is more traditional.

½ cup (1 stick) butter or margarine, softened
1½ cups sugar
1 teaspoon vanilla extract
2 eggs
1 tablespoon red food color
2 cups all-purpose flour
¼ cup HERSHEY'S® Cocoa
1 teaspoon salt
1 cup buttermilk or sour milk*
1½ teaspoons baking soda
1 tablespoon white vinegar
Fluffy Vanilla Frosting (recipe follows)

* To sour milk: Use 1 tablespoon white vinegar plus milk to equal 1 cup.

Heat oven to 350°F. Grease and flour two 9-inch round baking pans. In large mixer bowl, beat butter, sugar and vanilla until creamy. Add eggs and food color; blend well. Stir together flour, cocoa and salt; add alternately with buttermilk to butter mixture, beating until well blended. Stir baking soda into vinegar; fold carefully into batter (do not beat). Pour batter into prepared pans. Bake 30 to 35 minutes or until wooden pick inserted in center comes out clean. Cool 10 minutes; remove from pans to wire racks. Cool completely. Frost with Fluffy Vanilla Frosting.

10 TO 12 SERVINGS.

FLUFFY VANILLA FROSTING
½ cup (1 stick) butter or margarine, softened
5 cups powdered sugar, divided
2 teaspoons vanilla extract
⅛ teaspoon salt
4 to 5 tablespoons milk

In large mixer bowl, beat butter, 1 cup powdered sugar, vanilla and salt. Add remaining powdered sugar alternately with milk, beating to spreading consistency.

ABOUT 2¾ CUPS FROSTING.

TOLL HOUSE® DERBY PIE

The famous cookies, created by accident years ago at a New England inn called The Toll House, have become a sweet American institution and have spawned any number of equally chocolate-spangled treats. Naturally the folks at Nestlé®, who purchased the Toll House® name and made it famous, feel they own the chocolate chip franchise, and among the many variations on the theme they have developed, this blondie/cookie pie stands out.

2 eggs
½ cup all-purpose flour
½ cup sugar
½ cup firmly packed brown sugar
¾ cup butter, softened
1 cup (6-ounce package) NESTLÉ® Toll House®
    semi-sweet chocolate morsels
1 cup chopped walnuts
One 9-inch unbaked pie shell*
Whipped cream or ice cream

*If using frozen pie shell, use deep dish style; thaw completely. Place on cookie sheet; increase baking time to 70 minutes.

Preheat oven to 325°F. In large mixer bowl, beat eggs at high speed 5 minutes, until foamy. Add flour, sugar and brown sugar; beat until well blended. Blend in melted butter. Stir in NESTLÉ® Toll House® semi-sweet chocolate morsels and walnuts. Pour into pie shell.

Bake 1 hour or until knife inserted halfway between edge and center comes out clean, and top is golden brown.

Serve warm with whipped cream or ice cream, if desired.

MAKES 8 SERVINGS.

GILDING THE LILY: Despite the long association of walnuts and chocolate chips, I really prefer this pie when it's made with pecans. By way of accompaniment, ice cream is good, but coffee ice cream is better.

CHOCO-PEANUT BARS

These easy bars have a lot of different flavors and textures going on (the oats in particular are a nice touch), but the Baker's® chocolate is the essential ingredient. Labeled semi-sweet, it's always seemed to me to fall closer to the bittersweet end of the chocolate scale—a state of affairs that really suits my palate. The recipe also makes a lot of bars, which suits my appetite as well.

1 cup packed brown sugar
⅔ cup PARKAY® Margarine
1 cup peanut butter, divided
1 teaspoon vanilla
4 cups old fashioned or quick oats, uncooked
1 cup BAKER'S® Real Semi-Sweet Chocolate Chips, melted
1 cup coarsely chopped peanuts

Heat oven to 400°F.

Mix sugar, margarine, ¼ cup peanut butter and vanilla. Stir in oats. Press into lightly greased 15 × 10 × 1-inch jelly roll pan.

Bake 10 minutes; cool 5 minutes.

Stir together remaining peanut butter and chocolate; spread over crust. Sprinkle with peanuts.

Chill; cut into bars.

APPROXIMATELY 3 DOZEN.

MELTING MOMENTS

These meltingly tender little cookies have appeared on Argo® and Kingsford's® cornstarch boxes for over forty years. With only five simple, mostly nonperishable ingredients and a cool kitchen, they can be ready very quickly indeed (during hot weather it may be necessary to chill the dough before shaping the cookies). Over the years there have been many flavor variations (almond, anise, chocolate, coconut, mocha-cinnamon, orange, orange-clove, and pecan-cinnamon, to name most), but the vanilla-scented original recipe approaches ideal.

1 cup flour
½ cup ARGO® or KINGSFORD'S® Corn Starch
½ cup confectioners sugar
¾ cup MAZOLA® Margarine
1 teaspoon vanilla

In medium bowl combine flour, corn starch and confectioners sugar. In large bowl with mixer at medium speed, beat margarine until smooth. Add flour mixture and vanilla; beat until well blended. If necessary, refrigerate 1 hour or until easy to handle. Shape into 1 inch balls. Place 1½ inches apart on ungreased cookie sheets; flatten with lightly floured fork. Bake in 375°F oven 10 to 12 minutes or until edges are lightly browned. Remove; cool completely on wire rack. Store in tightly covered container.

MAKES ABOUT 3 DOZEN COOKIES.

ZEBRA BROWNIES

This recipe from Pillsbury illustrates one of the basic rules of back-of-the-box cookery: *The mix is only the beginning.* Of course you may make plain brownies from the Pillsbury Deluxe Fudge Brownie Mix, but if you fail to stir up the easy cream cheese–based zebra stripe mixture and marble it through the fudgy batter before baking, you'll have missed out on one of the tastier, more popular and more entertaining back-of-the-box recipes around.

FILLING
2 (3-oz.) pkgs. cream cheese, softened
¼ cup sugar
½ teaspoon vanilla
1 egg

BROWNIES
1 (21½-oz.) pkg. PILLSBURY Deluxe Fudge
    Brownie Mix
⅓ cup water
⅓ cup oil
1 egg

Heat oven to 350°F. Grease bottom only of 13×9-inch pan. In small bowl, combine all filling ingredients; beat until smooth. Set aside. In large bowl, combine all brownie ingredients; beat 50 strokes with a spoon. Spread half of brownie batter in greased pan. Pour filling mixture over brownie batter, spreading to cover. Top with spoonfuls of remaining brownie batter. To marble, pull knife through batter in wide curves; turn pan and repeat.

Bake at 350°F for 30 to 35 minutes or until set DO NOT OVERBAKE. Cool completely. Refrigerate at least 1 hour. Cut into bars. Store in refrigerator.

36 BROWNIES.

HIGH ALTITUDE—Above 3500 feet: Add ¼ cup flour to dry mix. Bake as directed above.

Recipe used with permission of The Pillsbury Company.

LEMON CHIFFON CAKE

The chiffon cake "technology," purchased from a Hollywood, California, baker, perfected by General Mills and marketed to sell their flour, was finally debuted to great excitement in 1948. It was the first really *new* cake type developed in many years, and not only did it surpass butter-based cakes and sponge cakes in lightness, tenderness and volume, it was easier to make. Based on a no-longer secret ingredient—vegetable oil—the cake was not only a windfall for companies such as Wesson and Mazola®, but since it was free of saturated fat, it was also (six egg yolks notwithstanding) remarkably modern. Over the years, endless flavor variations have been developed, but simple, classic lemon never fails to please.

2¼ cups sifted cake flour
1½ cups sugar
1 tablespoon baking powder
½ teaspoon salt
6 egg yolks
½ cup MAZOLA® Corn Oil
½ cup water
1 tablespoon grated lemon rind
¼ cup lemon juice
6 eggs whites, at room temperature
½ teaspoon cream of tartar

Into large mixer bowl, sift flour, sugar, baking powder and salt. Make well in center; add egg yolks, corn oil, water, lemon rind and juice. With mixer at medium speed, beat until smooth. In large bowl with mixer at high speed, beat egg whites and cream of tartar until *very stiff* peaks form. Gently fold flour mixture into egg whites until well blended. Pour into ungreased 10 × 4-inch tube pan. Bake in 325°F oven 65 to 70 minutes or until cake springs back when lightly touched.

Immediately invert pan over funnel or bottle. Cool completely. Loosen edges of cake with spatula. Remove from pan. If desired, glaze with Lemon Glaze (recipe follows) and garnish with very thin strips of lemon and/or orange rind.

MAKES 1 CAKE (14 TO 16 SERVINGS).

LEMON GLAZE
In medium bowl, stir together 1 cup sifted confectioners sugar, ½ teaspoon grated lemon or orange rind and 1 to 2 tablespoons lemon juice until sugar dissolves completely and mixture is smooth.

MAKES ABOUT ½ CUP.

GILDING THE LILY: Drizzle the glaze evenly over the cake. Good plain, the cake is simply splendid when accompanied by sliced, lightly sugared fresh strawberries.

BASIC BARBEQUE SAUCE

Actually, while this sauce appears basic, there's nothing ordinary about the flavor. It's offbeat, easy to whip up, keeps well and makes absolutely delicious chicken, spareribs, meat loaf or ham (brush often with the sauce near the end of cooking to build up a shiny, pungent glaze). As a fan of both molasses and mustard, I'm impressed by its three-ingredient simplicity and pleased to offer it in print. (The variations are nice, too, but try the basic sauce first.)

1 cup GRANDMA'S® Molasses
1 cup prepared mustard
1 cup vinegar

Mix molasses and mustard; stir in vinegar. Cover and refrigerate.

YIELD: 3 CUPS.

VARIATIONS

1. Tomato Barbeque Sauce:
Add 1 cup catchup to Basic Barbeque Sauce.

YIELD: 1 QUART.

2. Herb Barbeque Sauce:
Add ⅓ teaspoon each, marjoram, oregano and thyme to 1 cup Basic Barbeque Sauce.

YIELD: 1 CUP.

GILDING THE LILY: Use half best-quality, imported Dijon mustard and half imported grainy mustard for a deeper flavor and a more interesting texture. To make a sweeter sauce, add dark brown sugar to taste and simmer briefly to dissolve.

CINNAMON DATE NUT BREAD

The very idea of date nut bread is sweetly genteel and reassuring. There are dozens, probably hundreds of versions—some moister, some firmer— but they are nearly all good keepers and nearly all easy to make. They bespeak a time when there was always a simple little homemade something on hand. Sliced thin and spread with sweet butter or cream cheese, date nut bread is just right with tea or coffee when company drops in. Washed down with a glass of milk by the light of the refrigerator, it's also the perfect midnight snack.

3½ cups sifted flour
1 cup sugar
2½ tsp. baking powder
½ tsp. baking soda
1 tsp. salt
1 tsp. cinnamon
1 tsp. nutmeg
⅛ tsp. ground cloves
1 cup diced dates
½ cup chopped walnuts or pecans
1 egg, beaten
½ cup BRER RABBIT® Light Molasses
1¼ cups milk
¼ cup shortening, melted

Sift together flour, sugar, baking powder, baking soda, salt and spices. Add dates and nuts; mix well. Combine egg, molasses, milk and shortening. Add to flour mixture; mix until flour is moistened. Pour into greased 9×5-inch loaf pan. Bake at 350°F 1 hour 10 minutes or until toothpick inserted in center comes out clean. Cool in pan 10 minutes; turn out and cool completely on wire rack. Store in airtight container. Bread, stored overnight, will slice easier with serrated knife.

1 LOAF.

COOL 'N CREAMY COLESLAW

A wonderful discovery! Regular coleslaw is nice, but so *messy*, doncha know, which may or may not have been the thinking that led to this gelatine-based recipe, which produces coleslaw that cuts into tidy squares. Actually it tastes great and it *is* tidier, especially on a buffet, next to a big glazed ham, for example, or a smoked turkey.

2 envelopes KNOX® Unflavored Gelatine
2 tablespoons sugar
1¾ cups boiling water
1⅓ cups mayonnaise
¼ cup lemon juice
4 cups shredded cabbage
1 cup shredded carrots
¼ cup finely chopped onion

In large bowl, mix KNOX® Unflavored Gelatine and sugar; add boiling water and stir until gelatine is completely dissolved. With wire whip or rotary beater, blend in mayonnaise and lemon juice; chill until mixture is consistency of unbeaten egg whites. Stir in cabbage, carrots, and onion; pour into 11 × 7-inch pan and chill until firm. To serve, cut into squares.

MAKES ABOUT 8 SERVINGS.

GILDING THE LILY: My regular coleslaw always has a tablespoon or two of Dijon mustard, and so, now, does this one; blend the mustard in along with the mayonnaise and lemon juice.

MAPLE GLAZED SWEET POTATOES

There's nothing secret about maple syrup, but there is something mysterious about a natural food that, though it is produced in advance of spring, seems to taste so much of the fall and winter. Especially on the Thanksgiving table maple syrup makes an appearance, turning up in everything from the hot spiced cider cocktails that start things off to the deep-dish cranberry apple pie that is dessert. In between, it can also glaze the sweet potatoes, and by virtue of its unique flavor, give traditional marshmallow-topped sweets a real run for the money.

1½ pounds sweet potatoes or yams, cooked, peeled and quartered
½ cup CARY'S®, MAPLE ORCHARDS® or MacDONALD'S™ Pure Maple Syrup
½ cup orange juice
3 tablespoons margarine or butter, melted
1 tablespoon cornstarch
1 teaspoon grated orange rind

Preheat oven to 350°F. Arrange sweet potatoes in 1½-quart shallow baking dish. Combine remaining ingredients; pour over potatoes. Bake 40 minutes or until hot and sauce is thickened, basting frequently. Refrigerate leftovers.

MAKES 6 TO 8 SERVINGS.

SWEET AND SOUR CHICKEN

One obvious change in back-of-the-box cookery over the years is the growing number of ethnic recipes being published. As Chinese, Mexican and Italian trends have transformed our restaurant scene, so have they altered what we want to cook at home. Responding to the change, the corporate test kitchens have worked hard—some have even worked successfully—to create international recipes that retain authentic flavor, streamline and demystify the cooking process and utilize products that, for the most part, aren't authentically ethnic. The make-ahead stir-fry sauce base from Argo® /Kingsford® can be transformed into a number of Oriental-style dishes—none quicker or tastier than the following.

1 pound boneless, skinless chicken breasts, cut into strips
2 large green peppers, cut into 1-inch squares
2 medium onions, cut into ½-inch wedges
1 tablespoon MAZOLA® Corn Oil
1 cup Orient Express Stir-Fry Sauce (recipe follows)
¼ cup ketchup
1 can (8 oz.) pineapple slices, well drained and cut into eighths
⅓ cup sliced or slivered almonds

In 3-quart microwavable dish combine chicken, peppers, onions and corn oil. Microwave on HIGH (100%) uncovered, stirring once, 10 to 12 minutes or until chicken turns white; set aside. In 2-cup microwavable measuring cup combine sauce and ketchup. Microwave, stirring once, 4 minutes, or until sauce boils and thickens; pour over chicken. Stir in pineapple. Microwave 3 minutes longer. Sprinkle with almonds.

MAKES 4 SERVINGS.

ORIENT EXPRESS STIR-FRY SAUCE
In 1½-quart jar with tight fitting lid combine 2½ cups chicken broth, ½ cup ARGO® or KINGSFORD'S® Corn Starch, ½ cup soy sauce, ½ cup KARO® Light Corn Syrup, ½ cup dry sherry, ¼ cup cider vinegar, 2 cloves minced garlic, 2 teaspoons grated fresh ginger and ¼ teaspoon ground red pepper. Shake well. May be refrigerated 3 weeks.

MAKES ABOUT 4 CUPS.

PECAN PIE

The liquid sweetener that makes up most of the delicious goo in the filling of pecan pie can be varied according to your taste. Those who do not like the slight bitter edge molasses gives, but who want something a little different from the traditional dark corn syrup recipe, may wish to try this maple-flavored version from LOG CABIN®.

1½ cups LOG CABIN® Syrup
¼ cup sugar
¼ cup margarine
1½ cups pecan halves
1 unbaked 9-inch pie shell
3 eggs, slightly beaten
1 tsp. vanilla
Dash of salt

Heat oven to 375°F. Bring syrup, sugar and margarine to boil in saucepan. Boil gently 5 minutes, stirring occasionally. Cool slightly.

Place pecans in pie shell. Mix eggs, vanilla and salt in bowl. Gradually stir in cooled syrup. Pour over pecans. Bake 35 to 40 minutes or until knife inserted near center comes out clean. Cool.

MAKES 8 SERVINGS.

"PHILLY" POUND CAKE

A good pound cake is one of those simple, satisfying things that I, at least, can suddenly find myself craving at the most unexpected times. When life is complicated, and when the fancy things you're eating don't seem to be hitting the spot, a moist slice of this easy cream-cheese pound cake and a steaming cup of fragrant tea can give new meaning to the word *restorative*.

1½ cups granulated sugar
1 package (8 ounces) PHILADELPHIA BRAND®
  Cream Cheese, softened
¾ cup (1½ sticks) PARKAY® Margarine
1½ teaspoons vanilla
4 eggs
2 cups sifted cake flour
1½ teaspoons CALUMET® Baking Powder
Powdered sugar

Heat oven to 325°F.

Beat granulated sugar, cream cheese, margarine and vanilla at medium speed with electric mixer until well blended. Add eggs, mixing at low speed until well blended.

Gradually add sifted flour and baking powder, mixing at low speed until blended. Pour into greased and floured 9×5-inch loaf pan.

Bake 1 hour and 20 minutes. Cool 5 minutes; remove from pan. Cool completely on wire rack; sprinkle with powdered sugar.

MAKES 10 to 12 SERVINGS.

"PHILLY" PASTRY

Among pastries, few are easier or more reliable to make than this one. The results are always uniformly tender, and the cream cheese adds a welcome touch of tart flavor. This pastry is especially compatible with fruit fillings (it makes wonderful strawberry pie), but it can also be used to make small hors d'oeuvre turnovers that can be filled with ham, cooked sausage, mushrooms, cheese and so on.

1 package (3 ounces) PHILADELPHIA® BRAND
   Cream Cheese, softened
⅓ cup PARKAY® Margarine
1 cup flour
⅛ teaspoon salt

Heat oven to 400°F.

Beat cream cheese and margarine at medium speed until well blended. Add flour and salt; mix well. Form into ball; refrigerate.

Roll dough to 12-inch circle on lightly floured surface. Place in 9-inch pie plate. Turn under edge; flute. Prick bottom and sides with fork. Bake 15 minutes or until golden brown.

MAKES A SINGLE 9-INCH PIE SHELL.

VARIATION: For tart shells, divide dough into 24 balls; press into miniature muffin pan. Bake 10 to 12 minutes or until golden brown.

TIP: For long-baking pies, cover edges of crust with foil toward end of baking time to prevent excessive browning. If using pastry for filled 1 crust pie, bake pie according to directions for filling.

CLASSIC CRISCO® 9-INCH DOUBLE CRUST

First marketed in 1911, by soap giant Procter & Gamble, Crisco® failed to find ready acceptance. It was a new product (solid vegetable shortening) manufactured through a new process (hydrogenization), and American cooks and bakers (read: women) who had learned to bake with butter or lard were unimpressed. It took an extensive advertising and demonstration campaign by P&G, as well as World War–induced lard and butter shortages, before Crisco® began to win substantial converts. Now it's hard to imagine an American-style pie without at least a measure of Crisco® in the crust, and the following detailed formula was designed to remove as much of the pastry-making mystery as possible.

2 cups all-purpose flour
1 teaspoon salt
¾ cup CRISCO® Shortening
5 tablespoons cold water

1. Spoon the flour into a measuring cup and level with a straight-edged spatula. Combine the flour and salt in a medium bowl.

2. Cut in the CRISCO® shortening using a pastry blender (or two knives) until the flour is blended in to form pea-sized chunks.

3. Sprinkle with water, 1 tablespoon at a time. Toss lightly with fork until dough will form a ball.

4. Form the dough into one or two 5- to 6-inch "pancakes."

5. Flour "pancake" lightly on both sides.

6. Roll between sheets of waxed paper (or plastic wrap) on dampened counter top. Peel off top sheet. (Alternately, flour rolling surface and rolling pin lightly.)

7. Flip dough into pie plate, using the bottom sheet of waxed paper. Remove the waxed paper. (Alternately, trim rolled dough 1-inch larger than inverted pie plate. Loosen dough carefully. Fold into quarters. Unfold and press into pie plate.)

8. Add desired filling to unbaked pie crust. Roll top crust same as bottom. Lift top crust onto filled pie. Trim ½-inch beyond edge of pie plate. Fold top edge under bottom crust. Flute. Cut slits in top crust to allow steam to escape.

MAKES A DOUBLE 9-INCH CRUST.

LATTICE-TOPPED RAISIN PIE

Also called funeral pie in Pennsylvania Dutch country, raisin pie goes together quickly from pantry staples (if the death is sudden), is sweetly soothing (if the grief is overwhelming) and the filling is even mournfully colored (if you use dark raisins) to match the widow's weeds. Needless to say, you have to like raisins, but if you do, you'll adore this pie, and you won't want to wait until a special occasion (so to speak) to bake it.

3 cups DOLE® Raisins
2¼ cups water
¼ cup brown sugar, packed
2 tablespoons cornstarch
1 DOLE® Orange
1 DOLE® Lemon
2 tablespoons margarine
1½ teaspoons ground cinnamon
Pastry for 9-inch pie and lattice top

In saucepan, cook raisins, 2 cups water and sugar to boiling. Cover, simmer 5 minutes. Mix cornstarch with ¼ cup water; stir into raisin mixture. Cook, stirring, until boils and thickens. Remove from heat.

Grate 1 teaspoon peel each from orange and lemon. Squeeze 1 tablespoon juice each from orange and lemon. Add peel, juice, margarine and cinnamon to raisin mixture.

Pour filling into pie crust. Prepare lattice top. Bake in 425°F oven 30 to 35 minutes until filling begins to bubble and crust is golden. Cool 1 hour before cutting.

SERVES 8 TO 10.

ORANGE KISS-ME CAKE

This citrus-intense cake was the grand prize winner ($25,000) in the 1950 Pillsbury Bake-Off® Contest. Originally made with a food grinder (an entire chopped orange, peel and all, goes in), the cake fell out of favor as the usage of that low-tech appliance waned. In the Eighties, however, the rise of the food processor, which grinds the orange handily, brought the Kiss-Me Cake back into easy vogue. Moist and unfrosted (the baked cake is drizzled with fresh orange juice and sprinkled with a spiced nut mixture), it seems, even after forty-plus years, very modern.

CAKE
1 orange
1 cup raisins
⅓ cup walnuts
2 cups PILLSBURY BEST® All Purpose Flour
1 cup sugar
1 teaspoon baking soda
1 teaspoon salt
1 cup milk
½ cup margarine, softened, or shortening
2 eggs

TOPPING
Reserved ⅓ cup orange juice
⅓ cup sugar
1 teaspoon cinnamon
¼ cup finely chopped walnuts

Heat oven to 350°F. Grease and flour 13×9-inch pan. Squeeze orange, reserving ⅓ cup juice for topping.

In blender container, food processor bowl with metal blade or food mill, grind together orange peel and pulp, raisins and ⅓ cup walnuts; set aside.

In large bowl, combine flour and remaining cake ingredients at low speed until moistened; beat 3 minutes at medium speed. Stir in orange-raisin mixture. Pour batter into greased and floured pan.

Bake at 350°F for 35 to 45 minutes or until toothpick inserted in center comes out clean. Drizzle reserved ⅓ cup orange juice over warm cake in pan.

In small bowl, combine ⅓ cup sugar and cinnamon; mix well. Stir in ¼ cup walnuts; sprinkle over cake. Cool completely.

12 TO 16 SERVINGS.

SOCK-IT-TO-ME CAKE

There should be more of a story to go along with this recipe, but I'm sorry to say there isn't. It came to Duncan Hines® from the public domain in the late Sixties and it was surely inspired by the *Laugh-In* catchphrase of the day, but it cannot be reliably stated that Judy Carne baked one for Arte Johnson or that Lily Tomlin awarded it first prize at a telephone operators' bake-off or even that Duncan Hines® was a sponsor of that revolutionary television comedy program. Instead, thanks to the unusual name and the fact that the cake is delicious, it endures, like many back-of-the-box recipes, on its own popular inertia, making occasional reappearances on the cake-mix box and inspiring hundreds of consumer requests each year.

STREUSEL FILLING

1 package DUNCAN HINES® Moist Deluxe Butter
  Recipe Golden Cake Mix, divided
2 tablespoons brown sugar
2 teaspoons ground cinnamon
1 cup finely chopped pecans

CAKE

4 eggs
1 cup dairy sour cream
⅓ cup CRISCO® Oil or PURITAN® Oil
¼ cup water
¼ cup granulated sugar

GLAZE

1 cup confectioners sugar
1 or 2 tablespoons milk

1. Preheat oven to 375°F. Grease and flour 10-inch tube pan.

2. *For streusel filling*, combine 2 tablespoons cake mix, brown sugar and cinnamon in medium bowl. Stir in pecans. Set aside.

3. *For cake*, combine remaining cake mix, eggs, sour cream, oil, water and granulated sugar in large bowl. Beat at medium speed with electric mixer for 2 minutes. Pour two-thirds of batter into pan. Sprinkle with streusel filling. Spoon remaining batter evenly over filling, bake at 375°F for 45 to 55 minutes or until toothpick inserted in center comes out clean. Cool in pan 25 minutes. Invert onto serving plate. Cool completely.

4. *For glaze*, combine confectioners sugar and milk in small bowl. Stir until smooth. Drizzle over cake.

9

GOOD CANS

Canning, one of man's most important technological innovations, came about through Napoleon's need to carry food for his empire-building army over long distances. The winning result of a competition sponsored by the Emperor, the canning process spread rapidly through the civilized world, and people's lives were immeasurably changed as foods never before seen increased both their pleasure and their nutritional intake. Now we are in a time of reassessment, and some so-called improvements from the past seem more like mixed blessings. Processing removes vitamins, and refining all that aluminum contributes to pollution, and frozen foods somehow taste fresher and so on. Still, some ideas are just too good to disappear and so, for now at least, convenience wins out (and recycling is on the rise), and good cans fill our cupboards with all manner of delicious things to cook with—especially if there's a recipe on the label.

FAMOUS RO-TEL® CHEESE DIP

This regional product—diced or whole tomatoes canned together with green chilies—has been a Southwestern staple for years. Now that the label has been acquired by American Home Food Products, makers of such national brands as Chef Boyardee® and Gulden's®, and now that hot and spicy Tex-Mex food has become commonplace, perhaps Ro-Tel® will gain wider distribution. Certainly there's no easier way to arrive at chile con queso (hot cheese and chile dip), and if there's a back-of-the-package snack formula that could ever give Lipton's® Famous California Dip a run for the money in the quickness, simplicity and flavor departments, this is it.

1 (10 oz.) can RO-TEL® Tomatoes and Green Chilies
1 lb. pasteurized American Cheese

To 1 can RO-TEL® Tomatoes and Green Chilies add 1 lb. pasteurized cheese which has been melted in a double boiler (for additional thickness add more cheese). Mix together. Serve warm as dip with corn chips or crackers.

MAKES ABOUT 3½ CUPS.

SPAMBURGER™ HAMBURGER

In many homes (including the one in which I grew up) a sandwich of SPAM® Luncheon Meat, sautéed until hot and crisply browned, makes a quick and convenient supper (or lunch) meal. Those I ate as a child were fairly rudimentary—I recall meat, mayo and bread. Now the SPAMBURGER™ Hamburger, a new promotional recipe from Hormel Foods Corporation, takes things to a slightly more complex level, adding cheese, lettuce and tomato. Don't think of it as a sandwich that will replace the beef burger (crazy talk), but do enjoy it for a tasty change of pace.

1 (12-ounce) can SPAM® Luncheon Meat
3 tablespoons mayonnaise or salad dressing
6 lettuce leaves
2 tomatoes, sliced
6 slices American cheese
6 hamburger buns, split

GILDING THE LILY: Use honey mustard or barbecue sauce in place of, or along with, the mayonnaise.

Slice SPAM® Luncheon Meat into 6 slices (3 inches × ¼ inch). In skillet over medium heat, cook meat until lightly browned. Spread mayonnaise on cut sides of buns. Layer lettuce, tomato, meat and cheese on bun bottom. Cover with bun top.

SERVES 6.

PINEAPPLE UPSIDE DOWN CAKE

Pineapple, the most important cultivated tropical fruit, got its name from the Spanish for pine (piña), mistakenly bestowed because of its pinecone-like appearance. A New World native, it is now grown in many tropical climates, but thanks to the success of James Dole and the company he founded in 1921, the pineapple will always be associated with Hawaii. Because it should ripen on the vine for maximum flavor, and because when ripe it is then very perishable, Dole chose to can pineapple, eventually taking over most of the island of Lanai to feed the world's growing hunger for the sweet, juicy fruit. Improved shipping methods now mean that fresh pineapple is a market staple across the country, but canned fruit is still required in the following classic American cake.

⅔ cup margarine, divided
⅔ cup brown sugar, packed
1 can (20 oz.) DOLE® Pineapple Slices
10 maraschino cherries
¾ cup granulated sugar, divided
2 eggs, separated
Grated peel and juice from 1 DOLE® Lemon
1 teaspoon vanilla extract
1½ cups all-purpose flour
1¾ teaspoons baking powder
¼ teaspoon salt
½ cup dairy sour cream

Melt ⅓ cup margarine in 9-inch cast iron skillet. Remove from heat. Stir in brown sugar.

Drain pineapple, reserve 2 tablespoons syrup. Arrange pineapple in brown sugar mixture. Place cherry in center.

Beat remaining ⅓ cup margarine with ½ cup granulated sugar. Beat in egg yolks, 1 teaspoon lemon peel, 1 tablespoon lemon juice and vanilla.

Combine flour, baking powder and salt. Blend into creamed mixture alternately with sour cream and reserved 2 tablespoons pineapple syrup.

Beat egg whites to soft peaks. Gradually beat in remaining ¼ cup granulated sugar to make stiff meringue. Fold into batter. Pour over pineapple in skillet. Bake in 350°F oven 35 minutes or until cake springs back when touched. Let stand in pan on rack for 10 minutes, then invert onto serving plate.

SERVES 8.

SWISS STEAK DE LOMBARDI

Swiss steak in the house where I grew up was *always* white and creamy and, though we knew other families ate tomatoey red Swiss steak, we remained confident that our way (condensed mushroom soup) was the right way. As an adult, I now acknowledge that the very idea of "Swiss" steak, red or white, is an odd one. Surely not even the creamy version actually comes from Switzerland, and when you add tomatoes and mushrooms and attach a robustly Italian monicker, its pedigree is even less likely. I also acknowledge that when the food is good and convenient, such discussions of authenticity seem less interesting, so let's just get a batch of this whatever-it-is simmering and talk about something else. How about those Yankees?

1–1½ pounds top round steak, tenderized and
   cut into 4 serving pieces
Flour
Salt and pepper
3 tablespoons vegetable oil
1 can (14½ ounces) S&W® Italian Style Stewed
   Tomatoes, drained (reserve juice)
½ pound fresh mushrooms, sliced

Dredge meat in flour; season with salt and pepper. Heat oil in large skillet. Brown meat on both sides over medium-high heat. Pour reserved tomato juice over browned meat. Reduce heat to lowest setting and cover. Cook 1 hour or until meat is tender. Remove cover; add tomatoes and mushrooms. Cover and simmer another 5–10 minutes.

SERVES 4.

GILDING THE LILY: This dish can be baked in the oven at 350°F in a heavy skillet for the same length of time it cooks on top of the stove. I prefer to sauté the mushrooms in a little oil, along with a clove of chopped garlic, before adding them to the steak.

KRAUT CONQUERS ALL CHOCOLATE CAKE

I grew up in a family that loved sauerkraut. One great-grandmother in particular championed the tangy stuff, and when cool weather arrived, there was always a crock of kraut "working" in her cellar. Spareribs and sauerkraut was a favorite family dish (one, I note, to which Dagwood, a man who *knows* food, is also partial). Later, as a grown-up gourmet, I discovered choucroute garnie, the Alsatian dish of slowly braised kraut topped with multiple pork products, perhaps the ultimate expression of pickled cabbage. If sauerkraut hasn't conquered you yet, perhaps this recipe is the place to begin your initiation. Only slightly odder than cakes that include mayonnaise or canned tomato soup, this dark and fudgy double decker gains moisture and a coconut-like texture (but no real flavor) from what is, after all, a fairly modest measure of sauerkraut. This recipe comes from Steinfeld's®, a kraut packer in Portland, Oregon, but if their product doesn't reach your neighborhood, substitute another brand.

⅔ cup butter or margarine
1½ cups sugar
3 eggs
1 teaspoon vanilla
½ cup unsweetened cocoa
2¼ cups sifted all-purpose flour
1 teaspoon *each*: baking powder, baking soda
¼ teaspoon salt
1 cup water
⅔ cup rinsed, drained and chopped sauerkraut

Thoroughly cream butter with sugar. Beat in eggs and vanilla. Sift together dry ingredients; add alternately with water to egg mixture. Stir in kraut. Turn into two greased and floured 8-inch square or round baking pans. Bake in 350°F (moderate) oven 30 minutes, or until cake tests done.

GILDING THE LILY: Steinfeld's® suggests filling and frosting the cake with Mocha Whipped Cream or Chocolate Cream Cheese Icing; from this book you might wish to try the One-Bowl Buttercream Frosting on page 86.

SEAFOOD ENCHILADA CASSEROLE

With the appearance of this recipe on the back of Bumble Bee® tuna cans, the conquest of bland America by the zesty army of the Southwest seems complete. Where tuna noodle casserole, creamy and white, was once the symbol of the national weekday suppertime What To Eat, now Moms have alternatives like this lively, chile-spiked original. Almost as easy to make and every bit as satisfying but light years more *interesting* than that other casserole, it is a savory, vivid and welcome sign of changing times.

BUMBLE BEE®

1 can (12.5 oz.) BUMBLE BEE® Chunk Light Tuna
3 cups shredded Monterey Jack cheese
¼ cup diced green chilies
¼ cup diced green onion
½ teaspoon ground cumin
2 cans (10 oz. each) enchilada sauce
8 corn tortillas

Drain tuna. Combine tuna with 1 cup shredded cheese, chilies, onion and cumin. Warm enchilada sauce. Pour ½ cup sauce in bottom of 2-quart shallow casserole dish. Spoon equal amounts of tuna mixture into each tortilla. Fold sides to overlap. Turn seam-side down in casserole dish.

Pour remaining sauce over enchiladas. Top with remaining cheese. Bake in 375°F oven 10 minutes. Spoon sauce over enchiladas. Bake 10 to 15 minutes longer.

MAKES 4 SERVINGS.

GILDING THE LILY: The technique here is hardly rigorous, but you might simplify things even more by merely layering the ingredients to produce a lasagne-like dish. There are hotter and milder enchilada sauces, letting you regulate the heat to taste; using jalapeño Monterey Jack would also add more fire, if desired. Accompany the casserole with Refried Black Beans, page 68, and Mexicorn® Spoon Bread, page 117.

MEXICORN®
SPOON BREAD

I'm prepared to give pretty much any corn bread the time of day. I rarely find one, however dry and drab, that I can't at least butter into some kind of acceptability, and occasionally I run across a recipe, like the one for this casserole bread from Green Giant®, that makes a corn bread so flavorful and moist it needs no added embellishment at all. It's just right with chili or eggs or almost anything else plain corn bread is good with, and it's easy enough to make as a pure snack, enjoyed on its own.

½ cup margarine or butter, melted
1 (11-oz.) can condensed nacho cheese soup
1 (8-oz.) carton plain yogurt
¾ cup cornmeal
2 teaspoons baking powder
2 (11-oz.) cans GREEN GIANT® MEXICORN®
　　Whole Kernel Golden Sweet Corn with Red
　　and Green Sweet Peppers, drained
2 eggs, lightly beaten

Heat oven to 350°F. In 10-inch ovenproof skillet or 3-quart casserole, combine margarine, soup and yogurt; blend until smooth. Stir in cornmeal, baking powder, corn and eggs; blend well.

Bake at 350°F for 50 to 60 minutes or until knife inserted near center comes out clean. Serve warm. Store in refrigerator.

8 (1-CUP) SERVINGS.

GILDING THE LILY: OKAY, *a few* embellishments. A cup or so of finely chopped smoked ham will turn this into a main dish. Sliced green onions, chopped pickled jalapeños or mild green chiles will add additional Southwestern flavor.

Green Giant® and Mexicorn® are registered trademarks of The Pillsbury Company. Recipe used with permission of The Pillsbury Company.

GREAT BALL OF FIRE

The first trademark ever registered in this country was the red devil logo for William Underwood's canned deviled ham product; the year was 1867. Originally a Boston grocer, Underwood recognized the importance of canning very early and pioneered the method of manufacture in the U.S. Among his most popular products was a spiced, or deviled, ham mixture. The convenient meat spread suited America's love of portable food (the sandwich), not to mention its growing reliance on the lunch box and the brown bag, and it remains one of Pet® Foods' most popular products, even showing up, as this recipe proves, at party time.

1 cup (4 ounces) shredded Cheddar cheese
1 package (3 ounces) cream cheese, softened
1 can (4½ ounces) UNDERWOOD® Deviled Ham
2 tablespoons finely chopped green onions
3 tablespoons OLD EL PASO® Chopped Green
  Chilies
⅓ cup finely chopped walnuts
Crackers

1. In small bowl combine Cheddar cheese, cream cheese, ham, green onions and chilies; mix well.

2. Shape mixture into a ball. Roll in chopped nuts. Wrap in plastic wrap; chill.

3. Remove from refrigerator to soften slightly before serving. Serve with crackers.

MAKES 1 (2-CUP) CHEESE BALL.

GILDING THE LILY: Of course, I think this ball could use a lot more fire and would certainly use jalapeño Jack cheese in place of the Cheddar, and I might well add a chopped pickled jalapeño pepper or a few dashes of hot pepper sauce to the mixture before forming the ball.

OLD FASHIONED AMBROSIA PUDDING

S&W® Fine Foods first marketed the syrupy mixture known as fruit cocktail, an idea so good canners everywhere took it up. Turning the sweet mélange into easy desserts (as opposed to enjoying it straight from the can) was a logical extension of the concept's popularity. Such things as a mix cake baked with the fruit stirred into the batter are on the low-tech end of the cookery scale. This egg-thickened pudding-for-a-crowd, based upon the ambrosia salad idea, falls somewhere in the middle.

S&W Premium Quality Since 1896.

2 eggs, beaten
¼ cup sugar
2 cans (16 oz. ea.) S&W® Natural Style Fruit Cocktail, drained (reserve juice)
4 bananas, sliced and sprinkled with lemon juice
1 pkg. (16 oz.) miniature marshmallows
1 can (13.5 oz.) Crushed Pineapple, drained
1 can (3½ oz.) shredded coconut
½ pt. whipping cream, whipped

Whip cream; set aside. Cook eggs, sugar and reserved juices in top of double boiler until thick. Stir with wire whip. Cool. Fold into whipped cream. Meanwhile combine fruit cocktail, sliced bananas, marshmallows, crushed pineapple and shredded coconut in large mixing bowl. Blend whipping cream mixture into fruit. Cover and refrigerate at least overnight.

SERVES 12–15.

10

A TRIP AROUND THE KITCHEN

It's no wonder visitors from less "developed" countries are dazzled in American supermarkets. There are so many choices—too many choices, really—that it can seem hopelessly hard to make one's mind up what, if anything, looks good to eat. It's an overwhelming kaleidoscope of food, multiplied through the various combinations and permutations possible into a billion or so meals, all, if not delicious, at least edible enough to complete for our rather frazzled attention. In the vast selection, some stand out as more useful than others, and so here, as we close in on the end of this book, I have tried to make a selection of back-of-the-package recipes that produce dishes we want to eat from products we already buy. Make a trip around the kitchen, and you'll surely discover dried soup mixes and yogurt, graham crackers and gelatine already in the cupboard or refrigerator. So why shouldn't they become the secret ingredient in tonight's main course or appetizer or dessert?

CRAB CAKES

Old Bay® Seasoning, a seafood spice and herb mixture containing celery salt, mustard, bay, pimiento and ginger, among others, is a fifty-plus-years-old institution in the Baltimore area, and, increasingly, beyond. Around the Chesapeake, where the blue crabs are abundant, Old Bay® is the shellfish seasoning of choice. Whole crabs are steamed with it, and the coleslaw that goes alongside is pungent with the spice mixture, which gets stirred into the region's finest specialty: crab cakes.

2 slices dried bread, crusts removed
Small amount milk
1 tablespoon mayonnaise
1 tablespoon Worcestershire sauce
1 tablespoon Parsley Flakes
1 tablespoon baking powder
1 teaspoon OLD BAY® Seasoning
¼ teaspoon salt
1 egg, beaten
1 pound fresh lump crab meat

Break bread into small pieces and moisten with milk. Add remaining ingredients. Shape into patties. Broil or fry until golden-brown on both sides.

MAKES 4 SERVINGS.

GILDING THE LILY: The crab cakes make great sandwiches, served up on toasted buns. If you like OLD BAY® as much as I do, try stirring a little of it into some mayonnaise for slathering on your sandwich.

S'MORES

These easy treats are, by virtue of their three essential elements (graham crackers, chocolate bars, marshmallows), ripe back-of-the-box territory. Since they were supposedly invented by Girl Scouts, it seems to me that for proper flavor the marshmallows should be toasted over a smoky, open flame and for proper enjoyment the S'Mores should follow a strenuous upmountain hike and rousing campfire songfest. If you, like me, avoid outdoor living at all costs, here's an indoor variation from Nabisco® that will allow you to enjoy a batch of S'Mores without swatting a mosquito, climbing into a sleeping bag or washing your face in an icy stream. Sleep tight!

12 NABISCO® Graham Cracker squares
¼ cup CHIPITS® Semi-Sweet Chocolate Chips
12 CURTISS® Royal Marshmallows

Place graham cracker squares on baking sheet. Top each with several CHIPITS® Semi-Sweet Chocolate Chips and a CURTISS® Royal Marshmallow. Place under broiler just until chocolate is melted and marshmallow is browned. Serve immediately.

MAKES 12 COOKIES.

DELICATE GRAHAM CRACKER CAKE

Graham flour is an unsifted whole-wheat flour that includes the bran of the wheat kernel. Named for the Reverend Sylvester Graham, who believed in temperance and who set up Graham Hotels, which served healthy meals free from seasonings and stimulants, the flour was being made into something called a graham cracker as early as 1880. Today Nabisco® dominates the graham cracker market, and in addition to the millions used for S'Mores, in graham cracker crusts or eaten by Sophia from *The Golden Girls*, many more go into tender cakes like this one. Frost it with Hershey's® One-Bowl Buttercream Frosting (page 86) or use any favorite icing.

20 NABISCO® Grahams, finely rolled (about 1½ cups crumbs)
½ cup all-purpose flour
2½ teaspoons DAVIS® Baking Powder
½ teaspoon salt
½ cup BLUE BONNET® Margarine, softened
¾ cup sugar
2 eggs
1 teaspoon vanilla extract
¾ cup milk

In small bowl, combine cracker crumbs, flour, baking powder and salt; set aside.

In large bowl, with electric mixer at high speed, beat margarine and sugar until light and fluffy. Add eggs, one at a time, beating well after each addition. Stir in vanilla. Alternately add flour mixture and milk, beating well after each addition. Divide batter into 2 well-greased 8-inch round cake pans. Bake at 350°F for 25 minutes or until done. Cool in pans 15 minutes. Remove from pans; cool completely. Fill and frost as desired.

PORK CHOPS 'N PEACHES

Pork chops equal supper in many homes; hence the popularity of the coating mixes called Shake 'N Bake®, which produce a crisp crust, seal in the juices and add preseasoned predictability to something that shouldn't be so tricky but is (anyone who's ever been fed a bland, dried-out pork chop raise your hand). The trouble arises because modern pork is leaner than ever, a nutritional improvement that makes the cook's job harder and makes the sealing-in-the-juices function of Shake 'N Bake® critical.

1 can (29 ounces) peach halves*
8 pork chops, ½ inch thick**
1 envelope SHAKE 'N BAKE® Seasoning and Coating Mixture—Original or Hot 'N Spicy Recipe for Pork
¼ cup catsup
3 tablespoons brown sugar
2 tablespoons vinegar
2 teaspoons cornstarch

Heat oven to 425°F.

Drain peaches, reserving ½ cup syrup.

Coat pork chops as directed on package. Arrange in single layer in ungreased shallow baking pan.

Mix reserved syrup, catsup, brown sugar, vinegar and cornstarch; drizzle over pork chops. Bake 25 minutes. Place peaches in pan with chops; continue baking 5 to 10 minutes or until pork chops are cooked through. Spoon pan drippings over peaches. Serve pork with peaches.

MAKES 6 SERVINGS.

*Or use 1 can (20 ounces) sliced pineapple, or 1 can (17 ounces) chunky mixed fruit; moisten chops with water.
**Or use 6 pork chops, ¾ inch thick, and bake 30 minutes.

NILLA® CRANAPPLE CRISP

Crunchy crumb-topped fruit crisps, served warm, dolloped, perhaps, with a generous measure of heavy cream, are among winter's most satisfying desserts. (Summer's, too.) They're also among the easiest of desserts to assemble and combine fresh fruits and a few pantry staples into an easy formula that goes together in minutes. This cold-weather crisp is perhaps too homey to serve at Thanksgiving, but on another, less dressy occasion, sometime between, say, Halloween and the New Year, prepare this sweet treat for the family.

6 medium baking apples, cored, peeled and
   sliced
1 cup whole fresh or frozen cranberries,
   coarsely chopped
½ cup DEL MONTE® Seedless Raisins
6 tablespoons sugar
6 tablespoons BLUE BONNET® Margarine or
   BLUE BONNET® Butter Blend, softened
25 NILLA® Wafers, finely rolled (about 1 cup
   crumbs)
1 teaspoon ground cinnamon
⅓ cup PLANTERS® Pecans, chopped

In 2-quart casserole, combine apples, cranberries, raisins and ¼ cup sugar. Dot top of mixture with 2 tablespoons margarine or butter blend; cover. Bake at 350°F for 30 minutes.

Meanwhile, in small bowl, combine wafer crumbs, remaining 2 tablespoons sugar and cinnamon; cut in remaining margarine or butter until mixture resembles coarse crumbs. Stir in pecans. Uncover casserole; sprinkle with crumb mixture. Bake 15 minutes more. Serve warm.

MAKES 6 TO 8 SERVINGS.

CRISP CHICKEN DRUMSTICKS

Ritz® are the world's best-selling crackers, moving out of the Nabisco® warehouses at an astonishing rate. Obviously, Mock Apple Pie, one of the odder and more endearing back-of-the-box formulas, can account for only a small portion of the Ritz® enjoyed around the world. Instead, it is the buttery taste and crisp/tender texture that lead people to declare everything is better when it sits on a Ritz®. There is also a touch of class about this simple cracker, named, during the Depression, for the luxury hotel chain and meant to give its buyers a small thrill of affordable luxury. Here's another variation on the crispy-coated chicken theme (apparently a never-ending quest for those who cook from the back of the box), this one featuring my favorite part of the chicken.

24 RITZ® Crackers, finely rolled (about 1 cup
   crumbs)
¾ teaspoon salt
⅛ teaspoon ground black pepper
8 chicken drumsticks (about 2 pounds)
¼ cup all-purpose flour
1 egg, beaten
¼ cup BLUE BONNET® Margarine, melted

In medium bowl, combine RITZ® Cracker crumbs, salt and pepper. In plastic bag, shake chicken with flour; coat with egg, then with crumb mixture. Place in greased baking pan; brush with BLUE BONNET® Margarine. Bake at 375°F for 1 hour, or until tender

MAKES 8 SERVINGS.

CRISPY PORK CHOPS: Follow directions above using crumb mixture to coat 6 pork chops.

GILDING THE LILY: I don't think of one drumstick as a portion and believe this will likelier serve 4 diners, maybe even fewer.

PINEAPPLE LIME MOLD

Tourists always return home with shocking tales of some condition or practice that is common in a foreign land. Visitors to this country who head home can hardly complain about our telephones, friendly welcome, sanitary facilities, cheeseburgers or multiplicity of cable television choices. What, then, is left for defining how those barbaric Americans live? Well, they drive on the wrong side of the street, they have no-smoking sections in restaurants and all the wines are from California. Oh, and the Jell-O salads! Let me tell you, mon ami, about those salads . . .

1½ cups water, divided
1 package (3 ounces) JELL-O® Brand Lime Flavor Gelatin
1 package (8 ounces) PHILADELPHIA BRAND® Cream Cheese, softened
2 cans (8 ounces each) crushed pineapple, drained
1½ cups KRAFT® Miniature Marshmallows
½ cup chopped nuts (optional)
Shredded lettuce

Bring 1 cup water to boil; stir in gelatin until dissolved. Add remaining ½ cup water and juice.

Gradually add gelatin to cream cheese, mixing until blended.

Chill until thickened but not set; fold in pineapple, marshmallows and nuts.

Pour into 6-cup ring mold; chill until firm. Unmold onto serving plate; surround with lettuce. Serve with assorted fresh fruit and nuts, if desired.

MAKES 6 SERVINGS.

POLYNESIAN STUFFED CHICKEN BREASTS

One enduringly goofy back-of-the-box tradition is that of equating pineapple with all things tropical. Here that practice manifests itself in a recipe combining Stove Top® Stuffing, ginger and sweetly glazed chicken breasts, the kind of dish that, like something from Trader Vic's, would very probably be preceded by a Puu-Puu Platter and a couple of Mai Tais. It is artless and appealing (also easy to prepare), and seemingly exotic without being experimental enough to offend anyone. Good eating, in other words, even without the Mai Tais.

⅔ cup hot water
2 tablespoons margarine or butter
2 cups STOVE TOP® Chicken Flavor Flexible
  Serving Stuffing Mix
1 medium green pepper, chopped*
1 can (8¼ ounces) crushed pineapple in syrup
4 boneless skinless chicken breast halves
2 tablespoons brown sugar
2 tablespoons vinegar
¼ teaspoon ground ginger

Heat oven to 400°F.

Mix hot water and margarine in a bowl. Stir in stuffing mix, pepper and half the pineapple and syrup.

Place chicken between wax paper; pound about ¼-inch thick. Spoon stuffing evenly on chicken; roll tightly and secure with toothpicks. Arrange in 9-inch square pan; place any remaining stuffing in center of pan.

Combine remaining pineapple and syrup, sugar, vinegar and ginger. Spoon over chicken. Bake 30 minutes or until thoroughly cooked.

MAKES 4 SERVINGS.

NOTE: For split chicken breasts with bone and skin, follow recipe as directed above, placing ½ cup stuffing under skin of each chicken breast half. Bake 50 minutes or until thoroughly cooked.

*Or use ½ red pepper and ½ green pepper.

REFRIGERATOR PICKLES

Making pickles ranks right up there with weaving cloth and dipping candles as things most of us are unlikely to feel the urge to undertake. This country used to take pickles (an imported, English habit), more seriously than it does now, and there used to be fewer companies producing them for sale. In those days if you wanted a good pickle you had to make your own (or at least fish a few out of the barrel at the general store). If you're old enough to remember making homemade pickles, you'll remember they were a lot of smelly work; if you've never tried a homemade pickle, perhaps you're feeling curious about something good you've missed. Both of these population segments will welcome this easy recipe from Heinz® Consumer Test Kitchens, which goes together in minutes without cooking or canning and waits in the refrigerator until the right pickle moment—cold meat loaf sandwich, smoky country ham, big cheeseburger, Fourth of July picnic—arrives.

8 cups sliced unpeeled cucumbers
2 cups sliced onions
1 cup julienne red bell pepper strips
1 tablespoon salt
2 cups granulated sugar
1½ cups HEINZ® Distilled White Vinegar
2 teaspoons celery seed
2 teaspoons mustard seed

In a large bowl, combine cucumbers, onion and bell pepper. Sprinkle with salt and mix well. Let stand 1 hour. Drain. In a medium bowl, combine sugar, vinegar, celery seed and mustard seed; stir until sugar is dissolved. Place cucumber mixture in nonmetallic container. Pour vinegar mixture over cucumbers. Cover and chill for at least 24 hours to blend flavors.

MAKES ABOUT 8 CUPS.

NOTE: Pickles will keep in refrigerator up to 6 weeks.

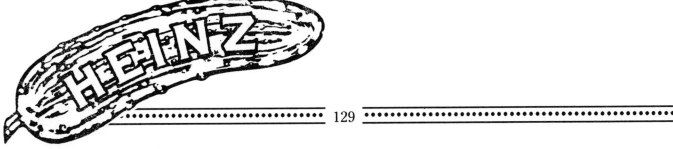

SAUSAGE AND PANCAKE BAKE

Jimmy Dean, the amiable country singer, has apparently found as much if not more success as the titular head of a sausage company than he ever did pickin' and singin'. The battle to sell high-fat foods in a low-fat world is apparently easier to win when plenty of old-fashioned country charm is applied to the pitch—marketing words of wisdom other companies might well heed. Jimmy's sausage is good fried up and enjoyed as is, maybe even better as the not-so-secret ingredient in this hearty breakfast casserole.

1 Pkg. JIMMY DEAN® Roll Sausage
2 cups pancake mix
1⅓ cups milk
2 eggs
¼ cup vegetable oil
2 apples peeled and thinly sliced
Cinnamon and sugar

Brown sausage in skillet. Drain. Mix pancake mix, eggs, milk, and vegetable oil together. Add sausage to pancake mix. Pour into greased 9"×12" casserole dish. Layer apples on top and sprinkle minutes. Serve with maple syrup.

SERVES 6–8.

GILDING THE LILY: Keep the sugar topping to a minimum, just enough to create a crunchy crust. The casserole can also be made with buckwheat pancake mix.

GOURMET GREEN BEANS

Bacon and cheese sauce will "gourmet" up almost any vegetable; thus, disguised green beans become a treat instead of a food group on a check-list. (Do I need to issue a disclaimer that there is no connection between this gooey production number and the magazine that goes by the same name? I think not.)

6 slices OSCAR MAYER® Bacon
¼ cup chopped onion
2 packages (9 ounces each) BIRDS EYE® Cut
   Green Beans, cooked, drained
1 jar (8 ounces) CHEEZ WHIZ® Pasteurized
   Process Cheese Spread
1 can (4 ounces) mushrooms, drained

Cook bacon until crisp. Drain bacon, reserving 1 tablespoon fat. Crumble bacon.

Cook and stir onion in reserved fat until tender. Add bacon and remaining ingredients; heat thoroughly, stirring occasionally.

MAKES 6 TO 8 SERVINGS.

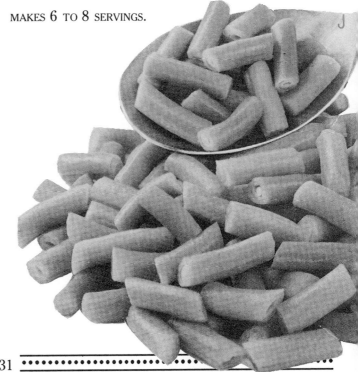

RED BEANS AND RICE

It's a measure of the renewed respect for quality sausages that the products of Hillshire Farm®, the Wisconsin company cofounded in 1929 by Austrian immigrant Fritz Bernegger, are now found in supermarket meat cases across the country. Kielbasa, bratwurst, spicy hot links and other succulent sausages—once the province of a dwindling band of various local artisan/butchers—are now welcome everyday staples. This rapido recipe, ready in only fifteen minutes, doesn't much resemble the New Orleans washday supper that inspired it (this is more Tex-Mex than Creole), but the speed with which it goes together certainly suggests it on a day when laundry or other chores prevent more elaborate cookery.

1 to 1½ lbs. HILLSHIRE FARM® Smoked Sausage
   or Polska Kielbasa, sliced
4 cups rice, cooked
2 16 oz. cans kidney beans
8 oz. can corn, drained
1 medium green pepper, chopped
1 jar salsa

Prepare rice. Sauté sausage slices until lightly browned. Add beans, corn, pepper, salsa; continue cooking until green pepper is tender-crisp. Serve sausage mixture over cooked rice.

SERVES 6.

COUNTRY HERB ROASTED CHICKEN

There are usually tremors in the back-of-the-box bedrock when a corporation tampers with either a product or a classic convenience recipe. Lipton's® recent renaming of its soup mix line, however, was accompanied by the information that the products themselves were unaltered. The new product titles ("Lipton® Recipe Secrets™ Savory Herb With Garlic Recipe Soup Mix," for example) may be cumbersome, but accurately reflect the simple fact that many more packages of these soups get stirred into recipes than ever get eaten as soup. This easy recipe, developed for the new name launch, is, says The Lipton® Kitchens, a classic-in-the-making.

2½ to 3 pound chicken, cut into serving pieces*
1 envelope LIPTON® RECIPE SECRETS™ Savory
    Herb With Garlic Recipe Soup Mix
2 tablespoons water
1 tablespoon olive or vegetable oil

Preheat oven to 375°.

In 13 × 9-inch baking pan, arrange chicken. In small bowl, combine remaining ingredients; brush on chicken. Bake uncovered 45 minutes or until chicken is done.

MAKES ABOUT 4 SERVINGS.

*Skinned, if desired.

GUACAMOLE

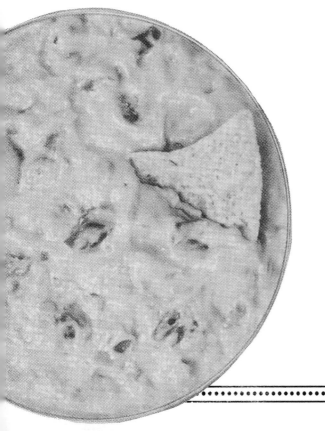

I've never had any leftover Lipton® California Dip (you know, the onion-soup-and-sour cream one), but I suppose it could happen. If so, this very Americanized guacamole is a fine way to extend it and get a second party out of a single batch of dip. For a crowd, of course, make the California Dip on purpose, preferably a day ahead, and double the guacamole. This simplified version of the great Mexican salad/sauce is particularly good atop a smoky grilled hamburger and wonderful on a baked potato.

1¾ cups mashed avocado (about 2 medium)
1 cup LIPTON® California DIP*
1 tablespoon lemon juice
¼ teaspoon hot pepper sauce

In medium bowl, combine all ingredients; chill. Serve with tortilla chips, green pepper wedges, tomato wedges or pitted ripe olives.

MAKES ABOUT 2½ CUPS GUACAMOLE.

*LIPTON® California Dip: Blend 1 envelope LIPTON® RECIPE SECRETS™ Onion Recipe Soup Mix with 1 container (16 oz.) sour cream; chill. Makes about 2 cups dip. (Cover and refrigerate remaining dip.)

VEGETABLE MEATLOAF

If meat loaf is your favorite meal and if chopping the vegetables for it your least favorite kitchen chore, this recipe from Knorr® could well become a suppertime staple. The soup mix adds a powerful dose of flavor and an interesting texture to a meat loaf that takes only minutes to assemble.

1½ pounds lean ground beef
1 package (1.4 oz) KNORR® Vegetable Soup and
  Recipe Mix
1 egg
½ cup seasoned dry bread crumbs
½ cup milk
Tomato sauce (optional)

In medium bowl combine first 5 ingredients. In foil-lined baking pan, shape beef mixture into 8 × 5-inch loaf. Bake in 350°F oven 1 hour. Let stand 10 minutes before slicing. If desired, serve with tomato sauce.

SERVES 4 TO 6.

GILDING THE LILY: If you do omit the tomato sauce, consider topping the loaf with about ⅓ cup ketchup, chili sauce or barbecue sauce.

GOLDEN CORN & GREEN BEAN BAKE

If it isn't broke, don't fix it, but if it can be spun off, go right ahead. A new soup from Campbell®, condensed golden corn, has led to this tasty (and very modest) renovation of that company's classic green bean bake. As a corn lover, I'm delighted with the flavor, and as a back-of-the-box connoisseur, I'm impressed by how much a simple change can transform a familiar old recipe.

1 can (10¾ ounces) CAMPBELL'S® Condensed
   Golden Corn Soup
½ cup milk
1 teaspoon soy sauce
Dash pepper
4 cups cooked green beans
1 can (2.8 ounces) French fried onions, divided

1. In 1½-quart casserole, combine soup, milk, soy sauce and pepper. Stir in beans and ½ of the onions.

2. Bake at 350°F 25 minutes or until hot and bubbling; stir. Top with remaining onions. Bake 5 minutes more.

MAKES 4½ CUPS OR 6 SERVINGS.

CAMPBELL'S is a registered trademark of Campbell Soup Company. Recipe provided courtesy of Campbell Soup Company.

SHORTCUT SLOPPY JOES

A second new Campbell® variety, Italian Tomato, has added many new possibilities to cooking with soup. Years ago my mother's sloppy joes were made with canned soup (Heinz® tomato, as I recall, which dates it well before the pickle company got out of the soup business), and while that recipe and this one don't resemble each other in the least, I welcome it by virtue of the nostalgia it arouses in me.

1 pound ground beef
1 can (11⅛ ounces) CAMPBELL'S® Condensed Italian Tomato Soup
¼ cup water
2 teaspoons Worcestershire sauce
⅛ teaspoon pepper
6 Kaiser rolls *or* hamburger buns, split and toasted

1. In 10-inch skillet over medium-high heat, cook beef until browned, stirring to separate meat. Spoon off fat.

2. Stir in soup, water, Worcestershire and pepper. Heat through, stirring occasionally. Serve on rolls.

MAKES ABOUT 3 CUPS OR 6 SERVINGS.

CAMPBELL'S is a registered trademark of Campbell Soup Company. Recipe provided courtesy of Campbell Soup Company.

Campbell's®

RICH LEMON BARS

Chocolate—what else?—wins the Favorite Dessert Flavor poll, but lemon lovers are a strong minority party, and many a chocolate champion would allow that a lemon dessert would do in a pinch. At the gourmet shop where I cut my culinary teeth years ago, the lemon bars were fragile and hard to pack—hard, even, to pick up—and the help was always choking on the cloud of confectioners' sugar that swirled around the attempt, but the bars nevertheless disappeared steadily, whether there were customers in the store or not. There are many versions; this one from Rea-Lemon® is a tangy, tender and reliable classic.

1½ cups plus 3 tablespoons unsifted flour
½ cup confectioners' sugar
¾ cup cold margarine or butter
4 eggs, slightly beaten
1½ cups granulated sugar
1 teaspoon baking powder
½ cup REALEMON® Lemon Juice from
    Concentrate
Additional confectioners' sugar

Preheat oven to 350°F. In medium bowl, combine 1½ cups flour and ½ cup confectioners' sugar; cut in margarine until crumbly. Press onto bottom of lightly greased 13×9-inch baking pan; bake 15 minutes. Meanwhile, in large bowl, combine eggs, granulated sugar, baking powder, REALEMON® brand and remaining *3 tablespoons* flour; mix well.

Pour over baked crust; bake 20 to 25 minutes or until golden brown. Cool. Cut into bars. Sprinkle with additional confectioners' sugar. Store covered in refrigerator; serve at room temperature.

LEMON PECAN BARS: Omit 3 tablespoons flour in lemon mixture. Sprinkle ¾ cup finely chopped pecans over top of lemon mixture. Bake as above.

LEMON COCONUT BARS; Omit 3 tablespoons flour in lemon mixture. Sprinkle ¾ cup flaked coconut over top of lemon mixture. Bake as above.

MAKES 24 TO 36 BARS.

OVEN-BARBECUED BEEF BRISKET

In Texas the local beef eaters prepare something called "Party Brisket." Clearly intended to duplicate the tender, smoky results of genuine cooked-over-wood barbecue—a slow, low and complex process that takes the know-how of a specialist—Party Brisket accomplishes in the oven, with the help of a splash of liquid smoke, what it would take a seasoned pit master hours and many pounds of hickory wood to accomplish. This brisket, which achieves the same barbecued results, is good sliced, but perhaps even better (although not as authentically Texan) served shredded, generously moistened with some of the sauce, piled on a toasted bun and accompanied by coleslaw and a chilled beer.

1 (5 to 6-pound) beef brisket
2 (15-ounce) cans tomato sauce
½ cup firmly packed light brown sugar
1 (3.5-ounce) bottle WRIGHT'S® Natural Hickory
    Seasoning
¼ cup A.1.® Steak Sauce
2 tablespoons lemon juice
½ teaspoon liquid hot pepper seasoning

Place brisket, fat-side up, in large roasting pan; set aside.

Blend tomato sauce, brown sugar, hickory seasoning, steak sauce, lemon juice and hot pepper seasoning; pour over brisket. Bake, covered, at 350°F for 4 to 5 hours or until tender, basting occasionally. If needed, thicken cooking liquid with flour; serve with sliced meat.

MAKES 8 SERVINGS.

GILDING THE LILY: I add 1 large onion, peeled and sliced very thin, to the tomato sauce mixture before baking the brisket. More hot pepper sauce won't hurt a thing, and the brisket can be prepared in a large brown-in-bag (follow the manufacturer's directions for preparing the bag).

SAVORY MASHED POTATOES

My current favorite mashed potatoes contain a generous measure of sour cream, whipped in just before serving. The results are luscious, rich and smooth, with a slight tang that is irresistible. Caution suggests that these potatoes are not everyday fare, however, and so in between high-cal batches of those spuds, I make these spuds, which manage to turn my major carbohydrate cravings into something approaching health food. We live in remarkable times.

1 tablespoon olive oil
1 tablespoon minced garlic
4 cups water
4 medium russet potatoes, peeled and cut into
    quarters (2 to 2¼ pounds)
1 cup DANNON® Plain Nonfat or Lowfat Yogurt
¼ cup milk
¼ cup sliced scallions or green onions
1 teaspoon salt
¼ teaspoon freshly ground pepper

In a large heavy saucepan or Dutch oven heat oil over medium-low heat. Add garlic; cook and stir 1 minute, stirring constantly, until fragrant but not browned. Add water and potatoes. Cover and bring to a boil over high heat. Reduce heat to medium-low and simmer 15 to 20 minutes or until potatoes are very tender. Drain well. Return potatoes to saucepan and mash. Add yogurt and milk and stir until creamy. Stir in scallions, salt and pepper. Serve immediately.

6 TO 8 SERVINGS (5 CUPS).

INDEX